1 MONTH OF
FREE
READING

at

www.ForgottenBooks.com

By purchasing this book you are
eligible for one month membership to
ForgottenBooks.com, giving you
unlimited access to our entire
collection of over 1,000,000 titles via
our web site and mobile apps.

To claim your free month visit:

www.forgottenbooks.com/free301358

ISBN 978-0-484-39394-2
PIBN 10301358

RECORDS

OF THE

NEW ENGLAND ASSOCIATION

OF

RAILWAY SUPERINTENDENTS

ORGANIZED IN BOSTON, MASSACHUSETTS
APRIL 5, 1848
DISSOLVED, OCTOBER 1, 1857

Printed by order of the Executive Committee of the
Eastern Railroad Association

WASHINGTON, D. C.
PRESS OF GIBSON BROTHERS
1910

A.247314

WASHINGTON, D. C., *April,* 1910.

At a meeting of the Executive Committee of the Eastern Railroad Association held March 10, 1910, attention was called to a manuscript book containing the original records of the "New England Association of Railway Superintendents," organized April 5, 1848, and dissolved October 1, 1857, which appears to have been the first railway association formed in this country having among its objects the protection of its members from unjust claims for infringement of patents. The book has been in the possession of the Secretary of the Eastern Railroad Association since early in 1875, when he obtained it directly from the widow of the Secretary who kept the records. It is therefore authentic, and contains much interesting information in connection with early railway matters, together with the names and signatures in facsimile of some of the leading pioneers in the railway business in this country.

Believing that the preservation in permanent form, and the possession of copies of this book would be appreciated, the Committee ordered a limited number of copies to be printed in pamphlet form for the use of the Association.

With the exception of the addition of indexes to facilitate the finding of names, or subject matter, the contents of the record book are herewith reproduced in original form.

JOHN J. HARROWER,
Secretary.

RECORDS OF THE "NEW ENGLAND ASSOCIATION OF RAILWAY SUPERINTENDENTS," ORGANIZED IN BOSTON, MASSACHUSETTS, APRIL 5, 1848; DIS= SOLVED OCTOBER 1, 1857.

After several informal preliminary attempts at organization a meeting was called on Wednesday, April 5, 1848, at the Revere House in Boston by the following invitation.

BOSTON, *March 29*, 1848.

DEAR SIR:

An association has been formed, which it is proposed should consist of the Superintendents and agents of rail roads in New England.

You are invited to attend its first meeting on Wednesday next, April 5th, at 8 P. M., at the Revere House and to become a member of the association if agreeable to you to do so when informed of its purposes and organization.

Refreshments (upon temperance principles) will be provided at the expense of the association.

William Parker, Supt. Boston & Worcester rail road.

Wm. Raymond Lee, Supt. Boston & Providence rail road.

Waldo Higginson, Agent Boston & Lowell rail road.

James Barnes, Supt. Western rail road.

Charles Minot, Supt. Boston & Maine rail road.

S. M. Felton, Supt. Fitchburg rail road.

This was sent to the following gentlemen, viz:

Messrs:

Onslow Stearns.

N. G. Upham.

Chs. F. Gove.

Josiah Hunt.

E. H. Brodhead.

Isaac Hinkley.

S. H. P. Lee.

Wm. A. Crocker.

George Haven.

Luther Haven.

Joseph H. Moore.

John Russell, Jr.

Of the above mentioned gentlemen there were present at this meeting:

Messrs. Onslow Stearns, Chs. F. Gove, Isaac Hinkley, S. H. P. Lee, Wm. A. Crocker, George Haven, Luther Haven, Joseph H. Moore, John Russell, Jr., and also Mr. Lucian Tilton, engineer of the Cheshire rail road, and Mr. Moore, engineer of the Vermont Central rail road, who were duly invited.

After some preliminary conversation, on motion of Mr. Lee, Messrs. Parker, Felton and Gove were appointed a committee to which, on motion of Mr. Crocker, Mr. Lee was added, to retire and report a plan of preliminary organization.

The committee retired and on their return reported as follows:

The committee appointed to nominate officers and devise ways and means for the organization of this association recommend:

William Parker, Esq., for President;

Chas. F. Gove, Esq., for Vice President;

Waldo Higginson, Esq., for Secretary.

The committee further recommend that Messrs.

William A. Crocker,

Samuel M. Felton,

Wm. Raymond Lee,

be a committee to prepare a constitution and bye-laws and report the same to the next meeting of the association.

This report was accepted and the officers and committee thus nominated were unanimously elected.

On motion the officers of the association were added to the committee.

The meeting then was adjourned to meet again at the Revere house on Wednesday, May the third, at 8 P. M.

WALDO HIGGINSON,

Secy.

WEDNESDAY, MAY 3D, 1848.

The second meeting of the association was held at the Revere house, May 3d, at 8 P. M.

Present: Messrs. W. R. Lee, Barnes, Minot, Felton, Higginson, Parker, Moore, Stearns, Hinkley, S. H. P. Lee, Crocker, Geo. Haven, Tilton, Hunt.

The committee appointed at the last meeting to draw up in writing a constitution, and code of bye-laws, reported the articles of Constitution prepared by them which were read and some amendments made, after which it was

Voted—

That the articles of Constitution as amended shall be the Constitution of this association.

It was then moved that the association proceed to the choice of officers under the permanent organization thus established.

Mr. William Parker declined a reelection as President.

Wm. Raymond Lee was then chosen President.

Chs. F. Gove reelected Vice President.

Waldo Higginson reelected Secretary.

Mr. Lee accepted the office to which he was chosen.

Mr. Gove was not present.

Mr. Higginson accepted the office of Secretary temporarily, but informed the association that he should resign as soon as an associate member was elected suitable for that office, which he stated could not in his opinion be properly filled by any of the immediate members living in Boston in consequence of their present avocations and the time required for its duties.

On motion of Mr. S. H. P. Lee it was

Voted—

That the officers of the association constitute a committee to prepare a code of bye-laws to be presented at the next meeting of the association.

On motion of Mr. Minot it was

Voted—

That the next meeting of the association shall be held on the first Wednesday in June.

On motion of Mr. William Parker it was

Voted—

That the President nominate a committee to procure a suitable place and to make arrangements for the future meetings of the association.

The President appointed as this committee:

Messrs.:

    Wm. Parker.

    Waldo Higginson.

    S. M. Felton.

Mr. Higginson nominated Mr. William P. Parrott as an associate member.

On motion of Mr. Felton it was

Voted—

That the Constitution be copied into a book by the Secretary and presented to the members for signature at the next meeting.

Voted—

To adjourn.

ARTICLES OF CONSTITUTION.

Adopted by the vote of the association, Wednesday, May the third, 1848.

ARTICLE FIRST:

This association shall be called the New England Association of Rail road Superintendents.

ARTICLE SECOND:

The objects of the association shall be the increase and diffusion of knowledge upon scientific and practical subjects connected with rail roads and the promotion of harmony among the rail road companies of New England.

ARTICLE THIRD:

It shall be composed of immediate and associate members.

Immediate members shall be persons filling the office or discharging the duties of rail road Superintendents in New England.

Any person may be chosen an associate member, whose connection with the association will tend to promote its objects.

ARTICLE FOURTH:

Persons to be elected members must be nominated at a regular meeting and balloted for at the next by the immediate members; an unanimous vote is necessary for a choice.

And the presence of as many as ten immediate members shall be necessary to constitute a regular meeting.

ARTICLE FIFTH:

The association shall be regularly organized with a President, Vice President and Secretary, who shall be chosen by ballot by the immediate members.

The President and Vice President shall be chosen from among the immediate members.

The Secretary may be chosen from either the immediate or the associate members.

The regular time for the choice of officers shall be at the annual meeting on the first Wednesday in January.

The officers for the present year shall be chosen at the meeting at which these articles of constitution are accepted.

The duty of the President and in his absence of the Vice President shall be to preside at all meetings of the association.

The duty of the Secretary shall be to keep a record of the

proceedings of each meeting and to preserve all papers and other property belonging to the association.

He shall have charge of all ordinary business transactions such as notifying members of meetings and making arrangements for the same.

He shall also act as Treasurer, collect all assessments and pay all bills of the association and make a report at the annual meeting of his receipts and expenditures.

ARTICLE SIXTH·:

Meetings shall be held at such times and places and for such purposes (in furtherance of the objects of the association) as shall from time to time be determined.

And assessments sufficient for the current expenses of the association shall from time to time be laid upon all members, payable quarterly.

ARTICLE SEVENTH:

Each immediate member shall be at liberty to introduce one stranger at any meeting of the association.

ARTICLE EIGHTH:

This constitution may be at any time amended by a vote of two-thirds of the immediate members.

The amendment having been proposed at the regular meeting previous to that at which it is voted upon.

ARTICLE NINTH:

Such of the following persons are to be considered original immediate members as intimate to the Secretary a wish to become so and sign the articles of Constitution within the present year.
Messrs:

Wm. Raymond Lee, Supt. Boston & Providence rail road.

James Barnes, Supt. Western rail road.`

Charles Minot, Supt. Boston & Maine rail road.

Saml. M. Felton, Supt. Fitchburg rail road.

Waldo Higginson, Agent Boston & Lowell rail road.

William Parker, Supt. Boston & Worcester rail road.

Joseph H. Moore, Supt. Old Colony rail road.

N. G. Upham, Supt. Concord rail road.

Chs. F. Gove, Supt. Lowell & Nashua rail road.

Onslow Stearns, Agent Northern rail road.

John Russell, Jr., Supt. Portsmouth, Saco & Portland rail road.

Isaac Hinkley, Supt. Providence & Worcester rail road.

S. H. P. Lee, Supt. Norwich & Worcester rail road.

Wm. A. Crocker, Supt. Taunton & New Bedford rail road.

George Haven, Supt. Fall river rail road.

Luther Haven, Supt. Cape Cod Branch rail road.

Lucian Tilton, Cheshire.

Josiah Hunt, Supt. Connecticut River rail road.

E. H. Brodhead, Supt. New Haven, Hartford & Springfield rail road.

WEDNESDAY, JUNE 7, 1848.

The third meeting of the Association was held agreeably to adjournment at the Revere house, this day, at 8 P. M.

Present:

Messrs. W. R. Lee, Parker, Russell, Hunt, Stearns, Haven, Crocker, Hinkley, Felton and Minot. ·

The Secretary being absent, Charles Minot was chosen Secretary *pro tem.*

The proceedings of the last meeting were read.

Mr. Parker, from the committee to provide a place of meeting, made a verbal report, that they had made arrangements to have future meetings held at the Adams House, and asked further time to report as to a room of resort.

Mr. Higginson, by letter, made his resignation of the office of Secretary of the Association.

William P. Parrott was chosen an associate member.

William P. Parrott was chosen Secretary of the association.

On motion of Mr. Felton,

Voted—

To lay an assessment of six dollars on each member.

On motion of Mr. Parker,

Voted—

That a committee of three be appointed by the President, to consider and report on the subject of draw and wheel springs and on car couplings.

The President appointed as this committee:

Messrs.

Parker.

Minot.

Hinkley.

On motion of Mr. Parker,

Voted—

That the President, Messrs. Crocker and Hinkley be a committee on the subject of track sprinkling.

Mr. Crocker nominated F. Amy, Supt. of N. Y. P. & B., as a member.

On motion of Mr. Parker,

Voted—

That Messrs. Higginson, Parker and Crocker be a Committee to prepare a list of periodicals to be subscribed for, and of books to be purchased, for the use of the association; and also to enquire into the best method of procuring detailed mechanical improvements from Europe.

On motion of Mr. Parker,

Voted—

That each member obtain authority from the Directors of his road, to represent them in a joint resistance to the application of Ross Winans for a modified renewal of patent, advertised in the public papers, including the employment of counsel, and to communicate the result to the President, Messrs. Minot and Higginson, who shall be a committee to act in accordance therewith.

That the Secretary communicate to each Superintendent now absent a copy of the above vote.

On motion of Mr. Parker,

Voted—

That when we adjourn, it be to the second Wednesday of July next, at the Adams House.

Voted—

To adjourn.

Attest,

CHAS. MINOT,

Secy pro tem.

WEDNESDAY, JULY 12, 1848.

The fourth meeting of the association was held at the Adams house in Boston, agreeably to vote of the last meeting this day at 8 P. M.

Present:

Messrs. Lee.

Higginson.

Gove.

Moore.

Crocker.

Hinkley.

Hunt.

George Haven.

Felton.

Luther Haven.

Stearns.

Tilton.

The meeting was called to order by the President.

The records of the last meeting were read.

The committee on the subject of draw and wheel springs and on car couplings called; not ready to report.

The committee on the subject of track sprinkler called; presented a written report, which was read and passed to the files of the association.   Accepted.

Committee on books and periodicals called; not ready to report.

On motion of Mr. Higginson it was voted that the committee on track sprinklers be requested to inform Messrs. Ross and Rutter that the compensation asked by them for the use of their improvement is in the opinion of this association a serious obstacle to its adoption.

On motion of Mr. Higginson it was

Voted—

That a committee be appointed to consider and report upon the expediency of the rail road companys in New England publishing a rail road gazette.

Mr. Higginson was appointed to act as this committee.

Mr. F. Amy, Superintendent of the New York, Providence and Boston rail road, was elected an immediate member.

Mr. Felton nominated Mr. T. Willis Pratt as an associate member.

Voted—

That when this meeting adjourn it be to the first Wednesday in August next, at 12½ o'clock, at the Union house in Springfield.

Voted—

To adjourn.

W. P. PARROTT,

Secy

FIFTH MEETING, AUGUST 2, 1848.

Agreeably to the vote at the last meeting the 5th meeting of the association was held at the Union House in Springfield this day at 12½ P. M.

Present:

Messrs. Parker.

Tilton.

Barnes.
Felton.
S. H. P. Lee.
Crocker.
Hinkley.
Hunt.

The President and Vice President being absent the meeting was called to order by the Secretary.

Wm. Parker, Esq., was elected President *pro tempore.*

Voted—

That the meeting be adjourned to 8 o'clock P. M.

At 8 P. M. the association met according to adjournment.

On call of report from committees,

The committee on car springs, &c., requested further time as they have not had sufficient time to perfect their report.

The committees on periodicals and rail road gazette did not report, none of the members of those committees being present.

Voted—

That the report on track sprinklers be recommitted with a copy of the vote passed the last meeting, to ascertain if the improvement is patented and if so to get the best terms upon which it may be used.

Voted on motion of Mr. Barnes—

That a committee be appointed to take into consideration the matter of the wear of rails and the best method of manufacturing the same.

The following gentlemen were appointed to be this committee.

Messrs.:

Crocker.
Felton.
Parker.
Barnes.

Voted on motion of Mr. Felton that there be a committee on patent questions.

The following gentlemen were appointed to be this committee:

Messrs.:

Lee.
Minot.
Higginson.

Voted on motion of Mr. Hinckley—

That the matter of Richard Imlay's claim of patent right in

the invention of transom couplings to trucks be referred to the committee on patent rights and that the Secretary send a copy of this vote to the members of said committee.

Voted—

That when this meeting adjourn it be to the first Wednesday in September, at the Adams House in Boston, at 8 P. M.

Voted—

To adjourn.

WM. P. PARROTT.

SIXTH MEETING.

In accordance with the vote at the last meeting the sixth meeting of the association was held at the Adams house in Boston, on Wednesday evening, September 6th, at 8 P. M.

Present:

Messrs. Lee.
       Parker.
       Minot.
       Luther Haven.
       Felton.
       S. H. P. Lee.
       Higginson.

The proceedings of the last meeting were read.

The committee on draw and wheel springs reported that valuable experiments are making and that their report should be deferred until the result of the experiments are known.

This report was accepted.

The committee on track sprinkling report that they have conferred with the patentees and return the former report with the reply of Mr. Ross to their questions.

Report accepted, and on motion of Mr. Parker was laid on the table.

Committee on rail road gazette reported a form which they recommend for the adoption of the association. Report accepted and laid upon the table.

Motion by Mr. Felton—

That there be a committee to take under consideration the matter of persons riding upon the engines, and to report some general rules and regulations for the same.

Messrs. Felton and Minot were appointed to be this committee.

Voted—

That when this meeting adjourn it shall be to the 1st Wednesday in October, at the Adams House in Boston, at ½ past 7 P. M. Adjourned.

WM. P. PARROTT,
Secretary.

SEVENTH MEETING.

Met according to adjournment, at the Adams house in Boston, Wednesday, October 4th, 1848, at 7½ P. M.

Present:

Messrs. Parker.
Minot.
Hunt.
Geo. Haven.
Felton.
Moore.
Stearns.
Higginson.
S. H. P. Lee.
Hinkley.

The President and Vice President being absent the meeting was called to order by the Secretary, and William Parker, Esq., was elected President *pro temp.*

The minutes of the last meeting were read by the Secretary.

The report of the committee on the rail road gazette was taken up and debated and recommitted with instructions to report a uniform code of general regulations for passengers to be printed with the different notices of trains and to be attached to the book in a conspicuous position.

The association then proceeded to ballot for the admission of Mr. T. Willis Pratt as an associate member.

Whole number of members present ten.

Whole number of votes for admission ten.

Mr. Felton for the committee reported upon the subject of "persons other than the engineman and fireman riding upon the engines" referred at the last meeting.

This report was accepted and it was unanimously

Voted—

That no persons, excepting conductors and master machinists, while on their own roads shall be allowed to ride on the engine unless by special permission of the Superintendent or some person to whom the Superintendent shall delegate that authority.

On motion of Mr. Hunt it was

Voted—

That there be a committee, of two appointed to report some rules to regulate the matter of employing men who have been discharged from other roads.

Mr. Hunt, Mr. S. H. P. Lee, appointed the Committee on this motion.

Mr. Hunt moved that the constitution be altered so that immediate members ceasing to act as Superintendents shall continue to be members as associate members.

Mr. Minot proposed Jas. Barnes, Esqr., as an associate member, he having ceased to act as the Superintendent of the Western rail road, having resigned that office.

Mr. Onslow Stearns proposed Mr. James Moore, Superintendent of the Vermont Central rail road, as a member.

Mr. Higginson proposed Mr. James N. Elkins, Superintendent of the Boston, Concord & Montreal rail road.

Voted—

That the next meeting of the association be held at the Adams house in Boston, on the first Wednesday in November, at 7 P. M.

WM. P. PARROTT,
Secretary.

The association met according to the appointment at the proceeding meeting on Wednesday, Novr. 1st, at 7 P. M.

The meeting was called to order by the President.

Present:

Messrs. W. Raymond Lee.

William Parker.

Tilton.

Stearns.

Minot.

Russell.

Felton.

Higginson.

Upham.

Hinkley.

S. H. P. Lee.

Luther Haven.

The proceedings of the last meeting were read by the Secretary.

Mr. Higginson moved—

That the minutes of the last meeting should be amended by

inserting the name of Mr. James N. Elkins, Superintendent of the Boston, Concord & Montreal rail road, proposed by him as an immediate member at the last meeting; and it was voted that the record should be so amended.

Voted—

On motion of Mr. Parker that the vote passed at the last meeting concerning the matter of persons riding on locomotives be reconsidered.

The following resolve was then proposed by Mr. Parker, and it was

Voted—

That we mutually recommend to each other the rule, that no one be allowed to ride upon the Locomotives attached to any train with the Engineman and Fireman; unless it be the Conductor or Master Machinist; so far as the said restriction may be practicable.

The President having engagements which required his absence from the meeting, W. Parker, Esqr., was chosen President *pro tempore*.

The several committees were called for reports; none being ready they were continued to the next meeting.

Voted on motion of Mr. Parker—

That a second assessment of ten dollars be laid upon each member of the association.

The association then proceeded to ballot for the admission of members.

Whole number of members present ten.

For James Barnes, Esqr., as an associate member there were ten votes.

For Mr. James Moore, Superintendent of the Vermont Central rail road, there were ten votes.

For James N. Elkins, Superintendent of the Boston Concord & Montreal rail road, there were ten votes.

The matter of a rail way gazette was then debated, upon the report of Mr. Higginson, and after some discussion referred to the next meeting.

Voted—

That this meeting adjourn to meet at ½ past six P. M., on Wednesday the 22d of November, at the Adams house in Boston.

W. P. PARROTT,

Secy

NINTH MEETING.

The association met according to appointment at the Adams house on Wednesday, November 22d.

Present:

Messrs. W. R. Lee.
 Chs. Gove.
 Minot,
 W. Parker.
 Luther Haven.
 Hinkley.
 Felton.
 Higginson.

No quorum being present the meeting was not formally called to order but after a general conversation upon rail road matters and after making the appointment for the next meeting at the Adams house in Boston on the Wednesday next preceding the last Wednesday (20th) in December, at 6½ P. M.

WM. P. PARROTT,
Secy

TENTH MEETING.

The association met according to appointment at the Adams house in Boston, on Wednesday, December 20th, 1848.

Present:

Messrs. W. Raymond Lee.
 S. M. Felton.
 Chs. Minot.
 W. A. Crocker.
 Onslow Stearns.
 J. Hunt.
 S. H. P. Lee.
 Jos. H. Moore.
 James Moore.   (9)

Meeting was called to order by the President. The minutes of the last meeting were read and approved.

Mr. Felton proposed for membership Mr. I. W. Stowell, Supt. of the Nashua and Worcester rail road.

Mr. Hunt proposed Mr. Henry Gray, Supt. of the Western rail road.

Mr. W. R. Lee proposed Mr. H. W. Nelson, Supt. of the Norfolk county rail road.

Mr. Felton proposed Mr. S. F. Johnson, Supt. of the Vermont and Massachusetts rail road.

Mr. Stearns proposed Mr. J. A. Page, Supt. of the Passumpsic rail road.

The chairman of the committee on patents reported verbally, that in the matter of Ross Winans' hearing before the commissioner of patents in relation to four wheel cars, able counsel had been employed to resist Mr. Winans' claim; that the result had not been communicated, but probably would be before the next meeting.

The committee upon the matter of men discharged from service upon rail roads, submitted a written report which was read and laid on the table, and upon a

Motion by Mr. Felton it was

Voted—

That the chairman of said committee cause fifty copies of the report to be printed and sent to the secretary for distribution among the members.

On motion of W. A. Crocker, Esqr., it was

Voted—

That the annual meeting be held at the Tremont house in Boston, at the time appointed by the Constitution (Wed. 3d of Jany., 1849) and that the President and Secretary be a committee to make the necessary arrangements.

Adjourned.

W. P. PARROTT,

Secy

FIRST ANNUAL MEETING

Was held at the Tremont house in Boston, on Wednesday the third day of January, A. D. 1849.

The meeting was called to order by the President.

Present:

Messrs. W. R. Lee.
        Chs. Minot.
        S. M. Felton.
        Jas. H. Moore.
        James Moore.
        W. A. Crocker.
        Jas. N. Elkins.

George Haven.

I. Hunt.

Onslow Stearns.

W. Higginson.

T. Willis Pratt.   (12)

The association then proceeded to ballot for president for the ensuing year. W. Raymond Lee, Esqr., had a majority of all the votes cast and was declared elected.

The association then proceeded to ballot for a vice president for the ensuing year and Charles F Gove, Esqr., having received a majority of all the votes cast, was declared elected.

The association then proceeded to ballot for Secretary for the ensuing year and W. P. Parrott was elected.

Messrs. Higginson and Minot were appointed as a committee to examine the accounts of the Secretary.

Committee on accounts reported that the Secretary's accounts are correctly vouched and cast, and said report was accepted.

The following persons were then chosen as immediate members having received the ballots of the whole number of members present viz:

I. W. Stowell, Supt. of the Worcester and Nashua rail road.

Henry Gray, Supt. of the Western rail road.

Henry W. Nelson, Supt. of the Norfolk county rail road.

S. F. Johnson, Supt. of the Vermont and Massachusetts rail road.

J. A. Page, Supt. of the Passumpsic and Connecticut Rivers rail road.

The subject of a rail road Gazette was taken up. On motion of W. A. Crocker, Esqr., it was voted that said matter be referred to the President and Mr. Higginson to report suitable rules for the government of passengers in the trains.

On motion of Mr. Higginson,

Voted—

That a committee be appointed to take under consideration the present form of State rail road reports and report such amend_ ments as may be conducive to a more perfect return and to report at the next meeting.

Messrs. Higginson, Parker, Felton appointed.

Mr. Hunt proposed Mr. Henry Farnum, Agent of the New Haven & North Hampton company, as an immediate member.

Voted—

That the next meeting be held at the Tremont house in Boston, on the Wednesday next preceding the last Wednesday in February, at 6½ o'clock P. M.

Voted—

To adjourn.

WM. P. PARROTT,

Secy

SECOND REGULAR MEETING, 1849.

Was held at the Tremont house in Boston on Wednesday evening, February 21st, 1849, at 6½ o'clock P. M.

Present:

Messrs. W. Raymond Lee.
Isaac Hinkley.
George Haven.
S. P. H. Lee.
S. M. Felton.
W. Higginson.
James Moore.
Chs. Minot.
H. Nelson.
L. Tilton.
W. A. Crocker.
W. Parker.
I. Russell.
I. W. Stowell.   (14)

Meeting was called to order by the President.

Mr. Minot proposed Mr. R. B. Mason, Supt. of the New York & New Haven road, as an immediate member.

Committee on rail road gazette and regulations of passengers and freight reported by Mr. Higginson.

It was moved by Mr. Parker that each regulation be read in order and the same was voted in the affirmative.

Article 1st was read and after some discussion it was voted that the same be adopted.

Articles 2d and 3d after discussion were adopted by vote nem. con.

Article 4th was divided and the first clause, to-wit: Passengers must not take nor leave the cars when in motion, was adopted. The other clause was discussed and the practice of using narrow platforms between the tracks considered.

It was admitted generally that the practice was bad.

Was considered necessary where trains stop to exchange passengers.   Instances mentioned on the Providence & Worcester
rail road, another on the Fitchburg road.   After some further discussion it was passed over.

Article 5th. It was moved to amend by striking out the word
"porter" and the same was accepted as amended.

After some discussion on the sixth article, it was voted on
motion of Mr. Higginson that the further consideration of the
subject be suspended and the report be printed and circulated
among the members.

On motion of Mr. Higginson that the proposed amendment of
the constitution be indefinitely postponed.

Committee on alteration of public rail road returns reported.

The report was accepted and it was

Voted—

That the same committee be requested to endeavor to get the
said report carried into effect by the Legislature.

The association then proceeded to ballot for Mr. Farnum as
immediate member.

The vote was not unanimous.

Mr. William Parker then renominated Mr. Farnum as an immediate member, and Mr. Charles F. Pond, Supt. of the Springfield
and New Haven rail road.

On motion of Mr. Minot it was

Voted—

That the committee on room confer with the society of civil
engineers on the subject of a joint occupancy of their room.

Voted—

That this association herewith regret that William Parker, Esqr.,
Supt. of the Boston and Worcester rail road, is about to leave
New England, and that a committee be appointed to tender to
him the compliments of the association as a token of the high
respect they entertain for him both personally and professionally.

On motion of Mr. Felton it was

Voted—

That a committee of seven be appointed by the chair to offer
to W. Parker, Esqr., the compliments of the association, he having made arrangements for leaving the Boston and Worcester
rail road to take the charge of the Baltimore and Ohio rail road,
and the said committee be authorised to make the necessary
arrangements for the same.

Messrs. Felton,   S. H. P. Lee,
       Crocker,   Higginson,
       Haven, Fall River,   W. R. Lee,
       Gove,

by request were appointed as said committee.

On motion of Mr. Stowell it was

Voted—

That a committee of three be appointed to take into consideration the subject of a standard time for rail roads and Messrs.
Stowell, Minot and Geo. Haven were appointed.

Voted—

That the next regular meeting be held at the Tremont House
in Boston on the Wednesday next proceeding the last Wednesday
in March, at 7½ o'clock P. M.

Third Regular Meeting, 1849.

The association met according to notice at the Tremont house
in Boston, Wednesday, March 21, 1849.

Present:

Messrs. Higginson.
       Isaac Hinkley.
       S. H. P. Lee.
       Jas. H. Moore.
       Upham.
       Geo. Haven.
       Minot.
       W. Parker.
       Hunt.
       Nelson.   (10)

The President being absent the meeting was called to order by
the Secretary.

Mr. Higginson was elected chairman.

The association then proceeded to ballot for Mr. R. B. Mason,
Supt. of the New York and New Haven rail road—

       Whole number of members.. ·· ·· ···   10
       Whole number of affirmative···· ···   10

The association then proceeded to ballot for Chs. F. Pond, Supt.
of the Springfield and New Haven rail road—

       Whole number of members present·· ····   10
       Whole number affirmative····· ···· ····   10

and for Mr. Henry Farnum, Supt. of the New Haven and North Hampton company—

    Whole number of members.   10

    Number in the affirmative.   10

Ordered that the Secretary procure a ballot box for the use of this association to be kept at the Tremont house.

The committee on rail road returns reported that they had attended to the same and that it was in the hands of the legislative committee.

On the motion of Mr. Hinkley it was

Voted—

That a committee of three be appointed to prepare and present an address to the different rail road directors upon the subject of contributing a room and library in Boston for the use of the association, and funds for the necessary expenses of the association.

    Messrs. Hinkley,

        Upham,

        W. R. Lee,

            Committee.

The consideration of the rules regarding freight and passengers was then taken up, considered and passed as follows:

In regard to Passengers:

Passengers must procure tickets before taking their seats in the cars.

They must not smoke in the cars or station houses.

They are not allowed under any circumstances to stand on the platforms of the cars.

They must not take or leave the cars when in motion.

Nor must they put their heads or arms out of the car windows.

Second, in regard to Baggage and Articles carried on the Passenger Trains:

All baggage must be delivered to the baggage master or other persons authorized to receive it before the passenger takes his seat in the cars.

Baggage must be accompanied in the same train by its owner; and when not so accompanied no agent of the company is authorized to put it on board the train; and the company will not hold themselves liable as common carriers in regard to it.

The liability of the company as common carriers in regard to baggage and other articles transported upon a passenger train, will not commence till such baggage or other articles are put or received on board the train, and the same liability will terminate when such baggage or other articles are unladen from the train at their place of destination.

Baggage will not be taken to include money, merchandise nor other articles than those of personal use; and when of higher value than the highest sum advertised by the company, notice must be given of that fact and an extra price paid or the company will not hold itself liable beyond that amount.

The company will not hold itself liable for any valise, package or other article of personal property taken by the passenger with him into the cars or carried at all upon a passenger train unless delivered to the baggage master or other person authorized to receive and take charge of such articles and no agent of the company is allowed to take charge of specie, drafts, bank bills or other small articles of great value to go by a passenger train unless it be specially advertised to the contrary.

The company expressly reject any liability for the care of articles in the keeping of express agents, who pass over their road under special contract, whether any such limitation of the company's liability is published in such express agents advertisement or not.

Third, as to Freight going by Freight Trains:

1. All articles of freight must be plainly and distinctly marked or they will not be received by the company.

2. The company will not hold itself liable for the safe carriage or custody of any articles of freight unless receipted for by an authorized agent; and no agent of the company is authorized to receive or agree to transport any freight which is not thus receipted for. Duplicate receipts ready for signing in the form prescribed by each company must accompany the delivery of any freight to that company.

1 x. Additional to rule No. 1:

And when designed to be forwarded after transportation on the rail road a written order must be given with the particular line of boats or teams marked on the goods if any such be preferred or desired.

No responsibility will be admitted under any circumstances to a greater amount upon any single article of freight than $200, unless upon notice given of such amount and a special agreement therefor. Specie, drafts, bank bills and other articles of great intrinsic or representative value will only be taken upon a repre-scutation of their value and by a special agreement assented to by the Superintendent.

The company will not hold themselves liable at all for any injury to any articles of freight during the course of transportation arising from weather or accidental delays.   Nor will they guarantee any special dispatch in the transportation of such articles unless made the subject of express stipulation.   Nor will they hold themselves liable as common carriers for such articles after their arrival at their place of destination and unlading in the company's warehouses or depots.

Machinery, furniture, stoves and castings, mineral acids, all liquids put up in glass or earthen ware, unpacked fruit, and live animals will only be taken at the owner's risk of fracture or injury during the course of transportation, loading and unloading, unless specially agreed to the contrary.

Gun powder, friction matches, and like combustibles will not be received on any terms, and all persons procuring the reception of such freight by fraud or concealment will be held responsible for any damage which may arise from it while in the custody of the company.

All articles of freight arriving at their place of destination must be taken away within twenty-four hours after being unladen from the cars. The company reserving the right of charging storage on the same or placing the same in store at the risk and expense of the owner if they see fit after the lapse of that time.

And the above regulations were adopted by the unanimous vote of all the members present, and the Secretary was ordered to cause the same to be printed as amended and duplicate copies to be sent to each member of the association with the request that each member should send to the Secretary in Boston, their assent or dissent to them, before the Wednesday next proceeding the last Wednesday in April next.

The association then proceeded to the consideration of a uniform method for certifying the discharge of men from the different roads.

And on motion of Mr. Hunt it was

Voted—

That the following form of certificate be adopted, viz:

NEW ENGLAND ASSOCIATION OF RAIL ROAD SUPERINTENDENTS.

Date————

Office of———— N.————rail road.

This certifies that Mr.———— N.————, has been employed on this road as———— (insert occupation) for————— (insert time employed) ending at date————.

And to conclude with a statement of the particular causes, if any, of the dismission or discharge.

And the certificate to be signed by the Superintendent.

Voted—

That the Secretary cause certificates printed in the form above described and send copies of the same with a copy of the report upon this subject with a request that they will notify him of their assent or dissent to the same.

And also the number of certificates required by each.

Voted—

That the next meeting of the association be held at the Tremont house in Boston, on the Wednesday next preceding the last Wednesday in April, at 6½ o'clock P. M.

Voted—

That a third assessment of ten dollars be laid upon each member of the association, and that the Treasurer collect the same.

Accepted.

WM. P. PARROTT,
Secy

FOURTH REGULAR MEETING, 1849.

The association met in accordance with the regular notice on Wednesday evening, April 18th, at 6½ o'clock P. M.

The meeting was called to order by the President.

Present:

Messrs. W. R. Lee.
   I. Hinkley.
   Chs. Minot.
   Nelson.
   S. H. P. Lee.
   Jos. H. Moore.
   Stowell.
   Higginson.
   Gove.
   Stearns.
   Felton.   (11)

The record of the last meeting was read and approved.

The Secretary was requested to draw up a code of bye-laws for consideration at the next meeting.

Voted—

That the matter of the rail road gazette be referred to Mr.

Higginson and that the same be published every other Monday, commencing on the first Monday in May.

Committee on the subject of preparing an address reported by their chairman, Mr. Hinkley.

Voted—

That the Secretary cause the same to be printed and a copy sent to each member of the association.

Committee on standard time for rail roads made a report which was read.

Voted—

That the same be recommitted to see what arrangements can be made for a standard time keeper.

Voted—

That the Secretary be requested to address every gentleman who has been elected a member of this association and has been duly notified thereof and who has as yet taken no notice of such election that unless a reply be received before the next meeting, it will be presumed that the gentleman thus delaying to reply declines becoming a member of the association and his election shall be considered void.

On motion of Mr. Higginson it was

Voted—

That an assessment of ten dollars be laid upon each member to defray the expenses of the complimentary dinner to Mr. Parker.

Mr. Gove was appointed in place of Mr. Parker on the committee on draw and wheel springs.

The following named rail roads have on or before the time of this meeting assented to the rules and regulations concerning passengers and freight and have agreed to adopt the same, viz:

> Boston and Lowell.
> Western.
> Boston and Providence.
> Providence and Worcester.
> Northern.
> Connecticut River rail road.
> Vermont Central rail road.
> Fall river.
> Boston & Maine.   (9)

Voted—

To adjourn to the usual time and place in May next.

     Approved.

WM. P. PARROTT,
Secy

SEVENTH REGULAR MEETING, 1849.

Was held according to due notice at Center harbor, New Hampshire, July 25th, 1849.

Present:

Messrs. W. R. Lee.
   Higginson.
   Upham.
   Gove.
   Minot.
   Tilton.
   Johnson.
   Hinkley.
   Russell.
   Stearns.
   Elkins.   (11)

The meeting was called to order by the President.

The record of the last meeting was read and approved.

The committee on bye-laws reported a form for the same, which after some discussion and alterations were adopted as follows:

BYE-LAWS OF THE NEW ENGLAND ASSOCIATION OF RAIL ROAD SUPERINTENDENTS.

RULE 1ST. The President shall take the chair and preside at all the meetings of the association and shall regulate and order all the proceedings.

RULE 2D. In case of the absence of the President, the Vice President shall perform all the duties of the President.

RULE 3D. In case of the absence of both President and Vice President, the meeting shall be called to order by the Secretary and the members shall choose one of their own number to preside at the meeting.

RULE 4TH. At all the regular meetings of the association the following order shall be followed in the transaction of business, unless it be set aside for the time being by vote of the members present.

The record of the last meeting shall be read and approved.

Candidates for membership to be proposed or balloted for.

Communications received since the last meeting to be announced and read if required.

Communications from the government of the association to be read.

Reports of committees to be called for.

Unfinished business if any.

Questions for debate if any to be discussed.

RULE 5TH. No member may speak more than twice on the same question; nor more than once, in any case, until every member desiring to speak shall have spoken.

RULE 6TH. All decisions of the chair on points of order shall be conclusive unless reversed by appeal to the meeting.

RULE 7TH. Every motion shall be stated distinctly by the President before debate, or taking the question; and every motion shall be reduced to writing if any member desires it.

RULE 8TH. When a question is under debate, no motion shall be in order unless for the previous question, to postpone indefinitely, to postpone to a day certain, to lay it on the table, to commit it, or to amend it.

A motion to adjourn shall always be in order and shall be decided without debate.

RULE 9TH. If required by any member the Ayes and Noes upon any question shall be called and entered upon the Journal.

RULE 10TH. The names of all members proposed shall be presented in writing with the name of the rail road of which they may be Superintendents, and in case of associate members the place of residence or post office to which communications may be sent.

The proposition to be signed by the member or members who present the candidate.

RULE 11TH. When any person shall have been elected member or associate member, the Secretary shall notify such person of his election, the time and place of the next meeting, and in case no answer is received within the period of two succeeding regular meetings, the election shall be deemed void.

RULE 12TH. Each member elected shall be held to pay all assessments which may be laid during the current quarter in which such election takes place; whether the same be laid before, or after the election.

RULE 13TH. Any person, immediate member, ceasing to act as a Superintendent of a rail road, shall be an associate member pro- vided that the association, at any regular meeting after he has notified the association of that fact, shall vote him to be an associate.

And any associate member elected a Superintendent of any rail road may be elected an immediate member at any regular meeting after due notice of said appointment.

RULE 14TH. All assessments shall be considered as due on the meeting next succeeding that on which the assessment is laid

And it shall be the duty of the Secretary to notify the amount of the assessment at the time of giving the notice of the meeting.

RULE 15TH. All committees shall consist of one and be appointed by the chair unless otherwise ordered by the meeting.

RULE 16TH. These bye-laws, may be altered, amended or added to at any regular meeting, ten members voting in the affirmative.

Provided, That notice of the proposed alteration shall have been given at a previous meeting.

The following gentlemen were then proposed for membership:

Mr. A. E. Swasey, Supt. of the Taunton branch rail road, by W. Raymond Lee.

Mr. B. C. Ruggles of the Connecticut and Passumpsic rivers rail road, address Wells river, by Onslow Stearns.

Mr. Thos. S. Williams, Supt. of the Sullivan rail road, by Chs. Minot.

Wm. A. Crocker, Esqr., of Taunton, as an associate member, by W. Raymond Lee.

The President having notified the association that Mr. Crocker has resigned his office of Superintendent.

A communication was made to the association by the President that the mortal remains of the late Colonel Whistler were on board a vessel which would probably arrive in Boston in the month of August.

Whereupon the following motion was made by Mr. Higginson.

Whereas, this association has learned that the remains of Geo. W. Whistler, Esqr., are soon to arrive at Boston, to be thence transported by rail road to their final resting place at Stonington Connecticut,

Resolved, that as a faint testimony of the love and respect entertained for the deceased, by all whose privilege it was to be in any way connected with him; and in view of the great services rendered by him to New England rail roads, a committee of this association be appointed to accompany his remains from Boston to Stonington.

The following gentlemen were appointed as this committee:

S. M. Felton, Fitchburg R. R.

N. G. Upham, Concord R. R.

W. A. Crocker, Taunton R. R.

Isaac Hinkley, Providence & Worcester R. R.

Josiah Hunt, Connecticut River R. R.

S. H. P. Lee, Norwich & Worcester R. R.
W. Higginson, Boston & Lowell R. R.

The committee on room reported that they had as yet made no arrangements. That seven rail roads had intimated their intention of contributing fifty dollars each for the support of the association, to-wit: Boston & Lowell, Boston and Providence, Lowell & Nashua, Fitchburg, Old Colony, Taunton branch, Providence & Worcester. After some conversation upon the whole subject it was on motion of Mr. Hinkley

Voted—

That the committee be instructed to report: at what price a suitable room can be obtained; the cost of fitting up the same for the use of the association; and what arrangements can be made for keeping it open and accessible to the members of the association at all times.

The committees on draw and wheel springs, on periodicals and standard time not ready to report.

Committee on gazette reported that an arrangement had been made with Mr.———— Snow; and that he is authorized to publish the same for the association, subject to such rules as may be given him from time to time.

Voted—

That the gazette be published once a month instead of twice a month, and the new publication to be issued the first Monday of each month.

To go into effect on the first Monday in September, and that the Secretary send Mr. Snow a copy of this vote.

The Ayes and Noes were ordered on this vote and each member present voted yes.

Voted—

That the committee on Gazette with the President be a committee to address a circular to rail road Supts. or Presidents calling their attention to the advantages likely to accrue to rail road companies and to the public from the rail road guide lately published under the auspices of this association, and urging upon them the importance of making to the publisher full and prompt returns of their running arrangements and suggesting the expediency of such details in the same as will render the various advertisements as uniform and full as is consistent with the different characters of the several roads and the size of publication.

Committee on wear of rails:

No report. W. P. Parrott was placed on the committee in place of W. Parker, Esqr.

Committee on sprinklers reported that the patentee will furnish the machines patent fee included for six wheels (2500 gallons) for 550 dollars; for eight wheels (3,000 gallons) for $650. Committee discharged.

On motion of Mr. Higginson it was

Voted—

That the committee on "Address" be instructed to send a circular to each Superintendent of roads which have not returned an answer to the former address, requesting them to signify to the association before the next meeting what may be depended upon for funds from their different roads.

On motion of Judge Upham it was

Voted—

That a committee be appointed to recommend to those roads included within the association that the fares of passengers be required to be paid and tickets taken prior to passengers taking their seats in the cars, except at those stations where tickets are not sold, and that the fares of passengers taken in the cars be established at an advanced price of five cents in all cases above the price of tickets sold at the office.

And that this committee confer with the different rail road companies and report at the next meeting what roads will agree to this regulation.

The following gentlemen were appointed on this committee:

Judge Upham.

Mr. Hinkley.

Mr. W. Raymond Lee.

The necessity of some rules in relation to lost baggage was introduced by Mr. Hinkley. After some discussion it was

Voted—

That a committee be appointed to draw up in form some rules for the better preventing loss to rail road companies from this source and present them for the consideration of the association at the next meeting.

Mr. Hinkley was appointed to this committee.

Voted—

That the next meeting be held on the Wednesday next preceding the last Wednesday in August, at such place as the President and Secretary may decide upon or at such other time in August.

. WM. P. PARROTT,

Secy

EIGHTH REGULAR MEETING, 1849.

The eighth regular meeting was held according to due notice at the Tremont house in Boston, on Wednesday, the 29th day of August, at 7 P. M.

Present:

Messrs. W. Raymond Lee.
   W. Higginson.
   S. M. Felton.
   S. H. P. Lee.
   Isaac Hinkley.
   Chs. Minot.
   I. Russell, Jr.
   Johnson.
   Tilden.
   Jas. Moore.
   I. Hunt. (11)

The meeting was called to order by the President.

Record of the last meeting was read and accepted.

The following gentlemen were then balloted for as immediate members and received the affirmative vote of each member present, to-wit:

Mr. A. E. Swasey, Supt. of the Taunton branch rail road, eleven votes affirmative.

Mr. B. C. Ruggles, Supt. of the Connecticut and Passumpsic rivers rail road, eleven votes in the affirmative.

Mr. Thos. S. Williams, Supt. of the Sullivan rail road, eleven votes in the affirmative.

W. A. Crocker, Esqr., as associate member, received eleven votes in the affirmative.

The following gentlemen were proposed as immediate members:

Mr. Genery Twichell, Supt. of the Boston & Worcester rail road, by Mr. Minot.

Mr. Solomon T. Corsen, Supt. of the Atlantic and St. Lawrence rail road, by Mr. Russell.

A communication was received from Robinson and company concerning a new rail road journal, which was read and after some discussion was laid on the table for further consideration.

A communication was received from Mr. Snow, the publisher of the rail road guide, which was read showing the receipts and expenditures and asking leave to use part of the book for advertisements.

Whereupon it was

Voted—

That the President be authorized to communicate to Mr. Snow the assent of this association to the insertion of a suitable number of proper advertisements, the suitableness to be decided by the President.

The Secretary reported the number of roads which have signified their assent to the rule requiring a higher rate of passengers when the fare is paid in the cars.

Nine roads have given a written assent. One gives its dissent from the rule; the other roads have given no definite answer, It was therefore

Voted—

That the committee be instructed to prepare a circular to the public to be presented at the next meeting which may be signed by the companies assenting to the same.

And to take such other measures as will bring the matter to a conclusion at the next meeting.

The committee upon lost baggage presented a report which was read and accepted.

Voted—

That the Secretary be authorized to cause the same to be printed and send a copy to each rail road in New England with the request that each road will inform the Secretary if they approve of the proposed arrangement and are willing to make the returns proposed.

The committee on the annual contribution reported, which report was read and referred back to the committee for the purpose of making further application to the roads from which no answer has been received and report at the next meeting of the association.

The committee appointed to prepare a circular upon the subject of the rail way guide presented an address which was read and accepted.

Voted—

That the Secretary cause the same to be printed and a copy sent to the President or Superintendent of each rail road in New England, with the request to each for a reply stating how far the object of the circular is approved and whether any or all of the four suggestions with which it concludes will be adopted.

Voted—

That the next meeting of this association be held at Brattleborough at the Vermont House, on the last Wednesday in September, at 6 o'clock P. M.

NINTH REGULAR MEETING, 1849.

The ninth regular meeting was held at Brattlebro, according to notice.

Present:

Messrs. Higginson,
      Hinkley,
      S. H. P. Lee,
      Felton,
      I. Russell, Jr.
      Tilton.
      Williams.
      Johnson.

No quorum being present the meeting was not called to order.

TENTH REGULAR MEETING, 1849.

Tenth regular meeting held at the Tremont house in Boston, on Wednesday evening, October 24, 1849.

Present:

Messrs. Lee.
      W. Parker.
      Higginson.
      Felton.
      Tilton.
      Williams.
      Hinkley.
      Swasey.
      Geo. Haven.
      Nelson.
      Stowell.
      S. H. P. Lee.
      Jos. H. Moore.   (13)

The minutes of the last meeting were read and approved.

Genery Twichell, Supt. of the Boston and Worcester rail road, was duly elected an immediate member of the association.

Mr. Felton nominated the Hon. Timothy Follett, Supt. of the Rutland and Burlington rail road, as an immediate member.

Mr. Johnson notified the association that he has resigned his office of Supt. of the Vermont and Massachusetts rail road.

The committee on room reported that they had engaged a room for the use of the association to be used by it as soon as the present occupant can find another room. The price, $250 per annum.

On motion of Mr. Felton it was

Voted—

That the committee on room be authorized to furnish the same with suitable furniture.

Committee on car and wheel springs. Mr. W. Parker reported that the car spring which he found in use on the Baltimore and Ohio rail road seemed to him to be the best he had seen, being simply an oak plank placed across the car near the middle and connected with the draw links by an iron rod passing the whole length of the cars.

Committee on circular to the several rail road companies in reference to funds for the support of the association returned the report recommitted at a previous meeting without alteration.

The committee on patents made a report on the subject of Tyler's patent safety switch, which after some discussion was laid on the table for further consideration.

The committee on standard time made a report recommending the time of a meridian, 2 minutes later than the meridian of Boston.

It was thereupon

Voted—

That this association recommend to all the rail road companies in New England the adoption (for this standard) of a time two minutes after the true time at Boston as given by Wm. Bond & Sons, No. 26 Congress Street, and that on and after the 5th of November, all station clocks, conductors' watches and all time tables and trains should be regulated accordingly.

Voted—

That the report and vote from the committee of standard time be printed in a circular and sent to each of the rail roads in New England, and that the same be inserted as an advertisement in the Pathfinder rail road guide, with the names of those companies as may have agreed to adopt the proposed standard.

Voted—

That the next meeting be at the usual time and place.

WM. P. PARROTT,

Secy

ELEVENTH REGULAR MEETING, 1849.

The eleventh regular meeting was held at the Tremont house in Boston, on Wednesday, Novr. 21, 1849, at 7 P. M.

Present:

Messrs. Lee.
      Nelson.
      Twichell.
      Higginson.
      Felton.
      Tilton.
      Swasey.
      Hunt.
      Hinkley.
      Williams.
      Minot.   (11)

The meeting was called to order by the President.

The record of the last meeting was read and approved.

Mr. Timothy Follett, Supt. of the Rutland and Burlington rail road, was elected an immediate member.

Mr. S. F. Johnson, late Supt. of the Vermont & Massachusetts rail road, was elected an associate member.

The President made a communication to the effect that Ross Winans had commenced an action against the Troy and Saratoga rail road company for an infringement of his patent for eight wheel cars and that Mr. Sargent, the Superintendent of that road, considered that he had a good defense.

The President suggested that it might be well to communicate with Mr. Sargent upon this matter and assist him if practicable in resisting Mr. Winans' claim.

Voted—

That the President be directed to communicate with Mr. Sargent upon this subject.

Ordered—

That the committee on the wear of rails be directed to prepare a circular to the several rail road companies to the end that the requisite information may be obtained from actual experience upon the different roads for the basis of a report upon that subject.

On motion of Mr. Higginson

Voted—

That a committee be appointed to prepare for publication before the next annual meeting a pamphlet containing the constitution of the Society and such reports of committees and other papers belonging to it as may be deemed worthy of preservation in a permanent shape, together with a brief notice of the history of the Society and a list of its officers and members.

On motion of Mr. Hunt

Voted—

That the rule be suspended and that a special committee of three be appointed by the chair for this purpose and

Messrs. Higginson,

Hunt,

Parrott,

were appointed to act as this committee.

Voted—

That the next meeting in December be at the usual time and place.

WM. P. PARROTT,

Secy

TWELFTH REGULAR MEETING, 1849.

The twelfth regular meeting was held at the Tremont house in Boston, on Wednesday the 19th of Decr., at 7 P. M.

Present:

Messrs. Lee.

Nelson.

Higginson.

Twichell.

Hinkley.

Stearns.

Hunt.

Minot.

Swasey.

Felton.

Williams.

S. H. P. Lee.

Tilton.

Russell.   (14)

The meeting was called to order by the President.

Record of the last meeting was read and approved.

Mr. Hunt proposed Mr. James P. Kirkwood, Supt. of the New York & Erie rail road, as a member.

Mr. Nelson proposed Mr. E. Noyes, Supt. of the Androscoggin & Kennebec rail road, as an associate member.

The Secretary presented a letter from Mr. Ashcroft accompanying a new proposed arrangement of safety plug; the communication was read, and Messrs. Minot and Parrott were appointed a committee to investigate the same, obtain terms for use of patent right and report at the next meeting if practicable.

The President presented a communication from Mr. P. B. Tyler, which was read.

The President stated verbally that the terms for using and making the patent switch of Mr. Tyler is fixed at ten dollars per mile.

This ratio was objected to by several members, as it would operate unfairly on several roads, and it was suggested that a price per switch would be better.

The whole matter was, therefore, referred back to the committee on patents, together with their former report on this subject.

With instructions to report the value of this switch as compared with the safety switch usually used in England and also to suggest to Mr. Tyler the expediency of fixing his price per switch instead of per mile or a less price per mile for long roads as compared with short ones.

The report of the committee on publishing the doings of the association was read and accepted and ordered to be printed.

Voted—

That the annual meeting be held at the Tremont house, and that the President and Secretary be instructed to make the necessary arrangements for the same.

Voted—

That the Secretary be directed to invite all the members of the Boston Society of Civil Engineers to meet with this association at their annual meeting on the first Wednesday in January next.

Adjourned.

SECOND ANNUAL MEETING.

Was held at the Tremont house in Boston, on Wednesday evening, January second, A. D., 1850.

Present:

Messrs. W. R. Lee.
   Russell.
   Nelson.
   Hinkley.
   Felton.
   Crocker.
   Swasey.
   Hunt.
   Stearns.
   Williams.
   Higginson.

Gove.

Haven.

Tilton.

Minot.

S. H. P. Lee.

Twichell.

Jos. H. Moore.　　　(18)

The meeting was called to order by the President.

The record of the last meeting was read and approved.

Mr. James P. Kirkwood was chosen an associate member.

Messrs. Sylvanus Bourne, Supt. Cape Cod branch R. R.; C. L. Schlatter, Supt. Ogdensburg R. R., were proposed, the first as immediate and the second as associate member.

Messrs. Higginson and Nelson were appointed by the chair a committee to audit the accounts of the Secretary.

Who reported the same to be correctly cast and vouched.

The association then proceeded to ballot for officers for this year.

For President:

W. R. Lee had the whole number of votes cast and was declared elected.

For Vice President:

Chs. F. Gove had the whole number of votes cast and was declared elected.

For Secretary:

W. P. Parrott had the whole number of votes cast and was elected.

The committee on publication reported the papers in the hands of the printer.

Committee on patents reported that they had written to Mr. Tyler, but in consequence of his absence had received no reply.

On motion of Mr. Higginson.

That the funds received from the subscription of the several rail road companies for the support of this association, be appropriated exclusively to the purpose of procuring and preserving books, models, recorded tables of statistics and such other information as may constitute a reliable basis for the solution of such problems in rail road management and construction as may properly come within the intent of this association.

Voted—

That the Secretary send a bill for the amount subscribed by each rail road company with a copy of the above vote.

On motion of Mr. Williams:—

That the constitution be altered so that the time for holding the annual meeting shall be the Wednesday next preceding the last Wednesday in January instead of the first Wednesday. Laid over by the rule.

Voted—

That the next meeting be at this place on the Wednesday next preceding the last Wednesday in February next.

WM. P. PARROTT,

Secy

SECOND REGULAR MEETING, 1850.

Was held at the Tremont house in Boston, Wednesday evening, Febry. 20th, 1850.

Present:

Messrs. Gove.

Higginson.

S. H. P. Lee.

Russell.

Hunt.

Stearns.

Nelson.

Tilton.

Twichell.

Williams.   (10)

Mr. Schlatter, Supt. Ogdensburg road, was elected an associate member.

Mr. Isaac H. Southwick was proposed as an immediate member by Mr. S. H. P. Lee.

Mr. Gove proposed Mr. George Stark, Engineer, as an associate member.

Mr. Isaac Hinkley proposed as an associate member, late Supt. Providence & Worcester R. R.

Voted—

That another committee be appointed upon the subject of lost baggage in place of Mr. Hinkley resigned.

Mr. Higginson appointed.   .

Voted—

That a circular be sent by the Secretary to each member request-ing a return before the next meeting to be held, March 20th, of the number, size, and description of wheels in use on his road, Jany. 1st, 1850.

1st. Number, size and description of driving wheels on engines.

2d. Number, size and description of other wheels including tender.

3d. Number, size and description of wheels under passenger cars.

4th. Number, size and description of wheels under freight cars. as far as practicable within the time specified.

The return to include only wheels actually in use under cars, and not those on hand and not in use. Each member is also to be requested to state what the practice is upon his road as regards the removal of cracked wheels from under the passenger and freight cars.

Voted—

That on and after the next meeting each member be requested to return to each meeting a statement of the number, size and description of wheels taken from under his engines, passenger or freight cars on account of cracks, breakage or from being worn by sliding on the rails during the month preceding that upon which the meeting is held and that the first return include both January and February of this year.

Voted—

That a copy of this vote be sent to each member by the Secretary.

Voted—

That hereafter models shall be presented to the association only by a member and shall not be accompanied by any person in charge of the same except by a special vote of the association, unless such person be an invited guest for the evening.

Voted—

That the rules and regulations adopted by this association be published in the Boston Daily Advertiser during the month of March, with the names appended of the roads which have adapted the same under the names signatures of the Superintendents and that the expense of the same be assessed upon said roads.

Voted—

That the Secretary be authorised to procure an engraved card showing a certificate of membership in this association.

To be signed by the President and Secretary.

WM. P. PARROTT,

Secy

THIRD REGULAR MEETING, 1850.

Third regular meeting of the association was held at their room, No. 11½ Tremont row in Boston, on Wednesday evening, March 20th, 1850, at 7 P. M.

Present:

Messrs. W. R. Lee.
   W. Higginson.
   S. H. P. Lee.
   Swasey.
   Nelson.
   Elkins.
   Jas. Moore.
   Felton.
   Twichell.
   Hunt.
   Upham.
   Moore.
   Tilton.
   Williams.
   Russell.
   Stearns.
   Kirkwood.
   Hinkley.   (18)

The meeting was called to order by the President.

The record of the last meeting was read and approved.

The meeting then proceeded to ballot on the admission of members and Mr. I. H. Southwick, of the Providence and Worcester rail road, was elected an immediate member.

Mr. Isaac Hinkley, of Lowell, was elected an associate member.

Mr. Sylvester Bourne, Supt. of the Cape Cod branch rail road, was proposed as an immediate member by Mr. Higginson.

Mr. Jn. N. Palmer, Supt. of the New London, Willimantic and Palmer rail road, as an immediate member, by S. H. P. Lee.

Mr. Liberty Bigelow, Supt. of the Rutland and Burlington rail road, as an immediate member, by Mr. Tilton.

Mr. Robert Hale, Supt. of the Conn. & Passumpsic rivers rail road, as an immediate member, by Mr. Williams.

A communication from Mr. Tyler in relation to the prices for his switch, was read and placed on file.

A communication from Mr. Higginson was read, by which it appeared that a valuable donation to the association had been made in books for the commencement of a library and also a portrait of the late Patrick T. Jackson, Esqr. It was thereupon *Voted*—

That the thanks of the association be presented to the officers of the Lowell rail road for their valuable presents.

Mr. Minot proposed Mr. Theodore Atkinson of the Manchester and Lawrence rail road as an immediate member and Mr. Edward Crane of Boston, as an associate member.

The committee on periodicals made a report which was read and placed on file and the Secretary instructed to confer with the govt. of the Boston Society of Civil Engineers in regard to a joint subscription and common use of books and periodicals.

Voted—

That the rules and regulations be published next month in the Daily evening traveller for one month.

Voted—

That the return of rails be committed to the committee on rails.

Voted—

That the returns of wheels be referred to Mr. Higginson.

The committee on patents by their chairman made a verbal report that Mr. Noyes' claim for patent on turn tables had been referred to Mr. B. R. Curtis for an opinion, who had stated that in his opinion the patent was valid. Upon the suggestions of Mr. Swasey further action upon this subject was deferred to the next meeting and Mr. Swasey was appointed a committee to obtain information upon the subject.

Voted—

That the returns of lost baggage (which has been on hand one week and upwards) be made to the Secretary on the 15th of each month.

A communication was received from Mr. M. C. Baker in relation to car couplings which was read and placed on file.

The committee for procuring a suitable room made their final report and were discharged.

WM. P. PARROTT,
Secy

FOURTH REGULAR MEETING, 1850.

Was held at the rooms of the association, 11½ Tremont row, Boston, Wednesday, April 17, 1850.

Present:

Messrs. Gove.

Hunt.
Higginson.
Southwick.
Tilton.
Williams.
Felton.
Minot.
Nelson.
Hinkley.
Twichell.
Haven.
Swasey.   (13)

The meeting was called to order by the Vice President.

The record of the last meeting was read and approved.

Voted—

That the balloting for admission of members be dispensed with on account of the lateness of the hour.

Mr. S. H. P. Lee notified the meeting through the Secretary, that he had resigned the office of Superintendent and he was nominated by Mr. Hunt as an associate member.

Mr. Higginson nominated Geo. M. Dexter, Esqr., of Boston, as an associate member.

A letter was received from A. Gilmore, Esqr., with a portrait of the late Major Whistler.

Voted—

That the same be accepted and the thanks of the association for the same be sent to Mr. Gilmore.

A report upon the comparative economy of wood and coal used in locomotive engines, was presented by Mr. Minot.

Voted—

That the same be accepted and printed and that Mr. Minot be a committee to cause the same to be done and to determine the number of copies.

The following rules were adopted in relation to lost baggage and the Secretary was directed to cause copies to be sent to each member of the association.

1st. All baggage unclaimed one week or upwards shall have placed upon each article in legible, permanent manner a number by which it shall after the first return be known.

2d. These numbers shall commence with No. 1 and the articles shall be marked by consecutive numbers for the whole year or until the sale of unclaimed baggage takes place upon the road.

3d. On the first of next month (May) a return shall be made of all articles thus numbered with as full a description of each article as is practicable.

4th. The succeeding returns shall be made of articles which may have collected for the time elasped since the last return, with their corresponding numbers, and of such articles as may have been claimed and taken away during the same time designating the latter by number only and to whom delivered.

5th. A fair record shall be kept in a book provided for the purpose at the office in Boston.

Several committees called and reported progress verbally.

Committee on lost baggage made as above a final report and was discharged.

Committee on wheels reported an abstract of the last returns and that they had prepared a form for future use.

Voted—

That said form be adopted by the association and that the Secretary furnish each member with fifty sets of the blanks for future returns.

Voted—

That a committee be appointed to ascertain from the Secretary the amount of bills paid or incurred by the association from the first with a specification of the same, of the class which in the opinion of the same are properly chargeable to the rail road companies, and also the amount to this time paid by said companies to the association, and the number and names of companies who have agreed to furnish $50.00 annually.

And said committee shall also recommend what steps if any are expedient to procure such additional aid from rail road companies as will be necessary to free the association from debt at this time, and whether any and if so what assessment is expedient on the members. And said committee shall be requested to report this evening.

The required information having been given by the Secretary, the committee reported that the amount properly chargeable to the rail road companies was $750.00.

The amount received and to be received from the annual subscription, $800.00.

The committee therefore reported that no additional aid is required from the rail road companies beyond the annual subscription.

That the amount properly chargeable to members is 978.52\frac{1}{2}$.

And that the unpaid assts. are $148.00 and that the sum of $362.52 is required to meet in full the obligations of the members.

The committee further submitted the following votes which were passed.

Voted—

That the Secretary send semi-annually, on the 1st of July and 1st of January, bills to each of the subscribing rail road companies for half the amount of said subscription.

Voted—

That the Secretary be requested to send a note to each of the subscribing rail road companies which has not paid its subscription for 1849, stating that he has been directed by the association to say that large expenses have recently been incurred in securing and furnishing their room, and respectfully ask their attention to their payment for the last year.

Voted—-

That the Secretary be requested to address a note to each member who has any subscription unpaid, stating the amount unpaid and calling their attention to the subject by direction of the association.

Voted—

Whereas, committees are often appointed by the association to examine inventions and other subjects during the intervals between meetings, and as the Secretary is often called upon to act upon these committees to the sacrifice of time and money, the association would hereby express their opinion of the propriety of his making a suitable professional charge to the patentee or other individual in interest for his time thus occupied, whenever he sees fit to do so.

Voted—

That the next meeting of the association be held at Taunton, Mass., on the Wednesday next preceding the last Wednesday in May.

FIFTH REGULAR MEETING, 1850.

Fifth regular meeting was held at the Taunton house in Taunton on Wednesday evening, — of May.

No quorum being present the association was not called to order.

SIXTH REGULAR MEETING, 1850.

The sixth regular meeting was held at the association room in Boston, on Wednesday the 19th of June. Chairman, Mr. Higginson.

Present:

Messrs. Higginson.
  Williams.
  Parker.
  Felton.
  Stowell.
  Upham.
  Twichell.
  Nelson.
  Swasey.
  Jas. Moore. (10)
Associates:
  Schlatter,
 · Pratt. (2)

Mins. of last meeting read and approved.

Sylvanus Bourne, Esqr., Supt. of the Cape Cod branch R. R., was elected an immediate member.

Theodore Atkinson, Esqr., Supt. of the Manchester & Lawrence rail road, was elected an immediate member.

Mr. Liberty Bigelow, Supt. of the Rutland & Burlington rail road, was elected an immediate member.

Mr. Robert Hale, Supt. of the Conn. & Passumpsic rivers R. R., was elected an immediate member.

Mr. S. H. P. Lee was elected an associate member.

Communication from Mr. S. H. P. Lee read and placed on file.

D. S. Jones, Esqr., Supt. of the Vermont & Mass. road, proposed by Mr. Felton.

On motion of Mr. Twichell it was

Voted—

That a committee of nine be appointed with full powers to take such action in behalf of the association as they may deem best with a view to perfecting the economical and reliable system of advertising adopted by the association in establishing the Path-finder railway guide.

Voted—

That the committee be appointed by the chair, and the following gentlemen were appointed:

The President, Mr. Lee.
  Messrs. Twichell.
    George Haven.
    Hunt.
    Felton.

Stearns.

Higginson.

Tilton.

Parrott.

Mr. Twichell presented a copy of Dr. Lardner's Railway Economy presented by John Edmonson, Esqr.; it was thereupon
Voted—

That the thanks of the association be tendered to Mr. Edmonson for his very appropriate present.

Judge Upham proposed an amendment to the fourth article of the Constitution, to substitute for the words an unanimous vote the words a vote of $\frac{3}{4}$ of the members present.

On motion of William Parker, Esqr.
Voted—

That the committee on patents be instructed to consider what alteration in the present patent laws is expedient for the protection of rail road companies.
Voted—

That the next meeting of the association be held at Gages Hotel at Bellows falls, on the Wednesday next preceding the last Wednesday in July.

WM. P. PARROTT,
Secy

SEVENTH REGULAR MEETING, 1850.

Seventh regular meeting was held at Bellows falls, on Wednesday, July 24, at 6 P. M.
Present:

Messrs. Felton.

Bigelow.

Atkinson.

Southwick.

Mason.

Russell.

Nelson.

Hunt.

Swasey.

Geo. Haven.

Bourne.

Williams.   (12)

The President and Vice President being absent the meeting was called to order by the Secy. and Mr. Felton was chosen chairman.

The record of the last meeting was read and approved.

D. S. Jones, Esqr., Supt. of the Vermont & Massachusetts rail road, was duly elected an immediate member.

E. H. Brainard, Esqr., Supt. of the Champlain & St. Lawrence rail road, was proposed as associate member, by Mr. Bigelow.

Mr. E. S. Chesbrough was proposed by Mr. Williams as associate member.

Mr. Henry Gray by Mr. Hunt.

A communication was received from Mr. Higginson in relation to advertising which contained an agreement which was signed by other members present and placed on file.

A model of a new rail road wheel, Wharton's patent, presented by the Secretary with some papers relating to the same.

The subject was referred to a committee consisting of
Messrs. Parrott.
   Williams.
   Hunt.

A communication was received from Mr. Pratt, atty. for Davenport and Bridges, calling the attention of the association to their claim for remuneration for use of a patent improvement in eight wheeled or other cars.

Referred, together with their letters patent, to the committee on patents:
Messrs. W. R. Lee.
   Minot.
   Higginson.

A model for a patented switch movement was presented by Mr. Williams.

Referred to a committee to report upon its merits.
Messrs. Williams.
   Nelson.
   Swasey.
   Haven.
   Bourne.
   Atkinson.

Mr. Southwick presented a model for an alleged improvement in switches; referred to the same committee.

Voted—

That the subject of Winans alleged patent right for eight wheeled cars be referred to the committee on patents with the request that they will obtain all the information that is to be obtained in relation to the late trial in New York and to report at the next meeting.

On motion of Mr. Hunt,

Resolved, that each rail road superintendent in New England be requested on the first day of every month to take measures to ascertain the numbers of all foreign merchandise cars on his road and report the same to the Superintendent of the road to which they belong.

Voted—

That the next meeting be held at New Haven, on the Wednesday next preceding the last Wednesday in August.

WM. P. PARROTT,

Secy

At the eighth and ninth meetings no quorum was present.

TENTH REGULAR MEETING.

The tenth regular meeting was held at Boston, on Wednesday evening, October 22d, 1850.

Meeting called to order by the President.

Present:

Messrs. Lee.
        Higginson.
        Moore.
        Russell.
        Hinkley.
        Southwick.
        Robt. Hale.
        Swasey.
        Tilton.
        Nelson.
        Bourne.   (11)

The record of the last meeting was read and approved.

Geo. M. Dexter, Esqr., was elected an associate member.

Mr. Tilton proposed Mr. D. A. Gage, Supt. of the Sullivan rail road, as an immediate member.

Mr. Higginson proposed Elbridge Harris, Supt. of the Bangor & Piscataquis canal and rail road Co., as an immediate member.

Mr. Swasey proposed A. S. Mathews, Supt. of the New York, Providence & Boston rail road, as an immediate member.

Mr. Lee proposed Professor D. H. Mahan, of West Point academy, as an associate member.

A communication from Mr. Elbridge Harris with a model of a car wheel construeted to guard against accident from the breaking of the axle was read and placed on file.

A communication from Mr. H. Tanner in relation to the patent lever brake, was read and referred to the committee on patents.

A communication from the President in relation to experiments on fuel for locomotive engines, was read and placed on file.

A model for an Horometer from Mr. Amos Abbott of Manchester, was presented and a letter from him concerning the same was read.

The Secretary was directed to reply to the same.

The Secretary read the report of the committee upon Mr. Ashcroft's safety plug. The same report was referred to

Messrs. Lee.

   Higginson.

   Felton,

and the Secretary to agree with Mr. Ashcroft upon terms for the use of the same and to determine upon printing the report.

Davenport & Bridges claim for the lateral motion to car trucks, was referred to the Secretary to report upon the subject after suitable examination at the expense of the association.

The committee on Wharton's wheels made a verbal report and ask further time for examination.

On motion of Mr. Higginson it was unanimously

Voted—

That the suppers hitherto provided for the association at the monthly meeting be hereafter dispensed with.

Voted—

That hereafter, in addition to the other occupation of the meeting, subjects be agreed upon at each for discussion at the next, and the subject thus adopted shall be stated by the Secretary in his notification.

Voted—

That the subject for discussion at the next meeting shall be: The profit and expediency of running excursion trains (similar to the "seven mile minor trains") at low prices.

       WM. P. PARROTT ,

        Secy..

ELEVENTH REGULAR MEETING, 1850.

The eleventh regular meeting was held at Boston, on Wednesday, Novr. 20th, A. D., 1850, at 7 P. M.

Present:

Messrs. Gove.

   Schlatter.

Jones.

Twichell.

Swasey.

Bourne.

Geo. Haven.

Hunt.

Hinkley. '

Williams.

Tilton.   (11)

The meeting was called to order by the Vice President.

The record of the last meeting was read and approved.

Mr. D. A. Gage, Supt. of the Sullivan rail road, was elected an immediate member.

Mr. Elbridge Harris, Supt. of the Bangor & Piscataquis rail road, was elected an immediate member.

Mr. A. S. Mathews, Supt. of the New York, Providence and Boston rail road, was elected an immediate member.

Professor D. H. Mahan, of West Point, was elected an associate member.

Mr. Thos. S. Williams proposed Mr. John Kinsman, Supt. of the Eastern rail road, as an immediate member.

The committees on Turner's patent and Davenport & Bridges, reported that the business in their charge was in progress but not finished.

The committee on Ashcroft's safety plug reported that in their opinion the sum of $12.50 per engine, twelve dollars 50-100, would be a suitable price for the apparatus including the patent right.

On motion of Mr. Higginson,

Voted—

That the Secretary prepare an abstract of the return of wheels and cause the same to be printed for the next meeting.

On motion of Mr. Hunt,

Voted—

That the next annual meeting be held at Springfield; that a committee of three be appointed to make suitable arrangements for the same and that the Supts. of rail roads in New York with such others as the committee may think best be invited as guests.

The committee appointed by the chair—

Messrs. Hunt.

Twichell.

Higginson.

On motion of Mr. Tilton,

Voted—

That a committee be appointed to take into consideration the subject of discussion for this evening and to present a report upon the same at the next meeting.

Committee: Messrs. Felton, Bigelow, Jas. H. Moore.

On motion of Mr. Hunt.

Voted—

That the association invite written communications upon the subjects of discussion at the meetings from members of the association.

It was agreed that the subject for discussion at the next meeting shall be:

The best mode or system for the examination of the wheels and axles of cars and engines, and which will afford the greatest security against accident from fracture.

WM. P. PARROTT,

Secy.

TWELFTH MONTHLY MEETING, 1850.

Present:

Messrs. Twichell.
Nelson.
Southwick.
Jos. H. Moore.
Williams.
Hunt.   (6)

No quorum being present the meeting was organized as a committee to consider the subject of the annual meeting.

Mr. Higginson was chosen chairman.

On motion of Mr. Hunt, it was

Voted—

That whereas, the rail road Convention of the northern lines is to be held at Boston, on the first week in January, and whereas, a large number of the members of this association must attend upon that convention. Therefore

Voted—

That the place of the annual meeting be changed from Springfield to Boston.

Voted—

That the committee of arrangements consist of
Messrs. Twichell.
        Higginson,
        Parrott.

WM. P. PARROTT,
Secy.

THE THIRD ANNUAL MEETING.

Was held at the rooms of the association in Boston, on Wednesday evening, Jany. 1st, A. D., 1851.

Present:

Messrs. Higginson.
        Williams.
        Stearns.
        Atkinson.
        Hunt.
        Gale.
        Hale.
        Swasey.
        Southwick.
        Hinkley.
        Jas. Moore.
        Jos. H. Moore.   (12)

The President and Vice President being absent the meeting was called to order by the Secretary.

Mr. Higginson was chosen chairman.

The record of the last meeting was read and approved.

Messrs. Williams and Stearns were appointed a committee to examine the accounts of the association for the past year.

Mr. John Kinsman, Supt. of the Eastern rail road, was chosen an immediate member of the association.

Mr. Williams proposed James Sweetsir, Supt. of the Portland, Portsmouth & Saco rail road, D. N. Pickering, Supt. of the South Reading branch and Wm. Merritt, Supt. of the Essex rail road, as immediate members.

Mr. Swasey proposed Mr. E. H. Brodhead, Supt. of the Hartford, Providence and Fishkill rail road, as an immediate member.

The committee on accounts reported that the same were properly vouched and cast.

The association then proceeded to the choice of officers for the ensuing year.

Mr. Swasey was appointed to collect and count the votes.

The votes for President were—

Ten (10) for W. Raymond Lee, who was declared elected President of the association for the present year.

The votes for Vice President were—

Ten (10) for Chs. F. Gove, who was declared elected Vice President of the association for the ensuing year.

The votes for Secretary were—

Ten (10) for Wm. P. Parrott, who was elected Secretary.

Voted—

That in consequence of the lateness of the hour and the other engagements of the association the other business before the association be postponed to the next meeting.

Voted—

To adjourn.

WM. P. PARROTT,

Secy.

FIRST MONTHLY MEETING, JANUARY 29, 1851.

Present:

Messrs. Lee.
   Stearns.
   Felton.
   Gage.
   Hale.
   Jas. Moore.
   Williams.
   Southwick.
   Bigelow.
   Jos. H. Moore.
   Hinkley.
   Tilton. (12)

Record of the last meeting was read and approved.

The following gentlemen proposed at the last meeting were elected immediate members, viz:

Messrs. Sweetsir.
   Pickering.
   Merritt.
   Brodhead.

The Secretary made reports upon the matter of Davenport & Bridges patent side motion, Turner's patent break, also report upon the abstract of the returns of broken wheels.

Voted—

That the subject of the returns of wheels be referred to the President and Secretary to report at the next meeting.

Mr. S. T. Corser, Supt. of the Atlantic and St. Lawrence rail road, was proposed as an immediate member.

Voted—

That the Secretary be directed to examine the claim of Mr. Kimball for a patent method of hanging breaks for cars.

Voted—

That an assessment of ten dollars be assessed on each member for the year 1850, and the Secretary be directed to collect the same.

The association then proceeded to discuss the subject proposed at the last meeting in 1850, viz: "The best method for daily examination of wheels and axles."

Voted—

That the subject for discussion at the next meeting be "The subject of ticket accountability."

WM. P. PARROTT,

Secy.

SECOND MONTHLY MEETING, FEBY. 19TH, 1851.

Present:

Messrs. Lee.
      Gove.
      Higginson.
      Moore.
      Hale.
      Tilton.
      Gage.
      Twichell.
      Bourne.
      Southwick.
      Swasey.
      Williams.
      Stearns.
      Nelson.   (14)

The record of the last meeting was read and approved.

Mr. S. T. Corser, Supt. of the Atlantic and St. Lawrence rail road, was elected an immediate member.

Mr. Wm. L. Dearborn presented to the association by the Secretary a box of danger signals imported by him from England for the purpose of experimenting with them in order to determine their usefulness.

Voted—

That the thanks of the association be given to Mr. Dearborn for his present, and experiments be made with them on the afternoon preceding the evening of the next meeting on the Lowell rail road, at the Boston station, at 4 P. M., and that notice of the same be given in the notice of the meeting.

A model of a patented slide table was presented by the Secretary; after some remarks by the President the subject was referred to the next meeting.

Voted—

That the Secretary be authorized to subscribe for the Mechanics magazine, published by Appleton, New York.

Verbal report was made upon the subject of Kimball's patent and the subject was referred to the next meeting.

The report of the committee appointed at the last meeting to examine the subject of wheel returns, was taken up upon verbal report. After some remarks upon the subject by the President and Mr. Higginson, the further report was deferred to the next meeting.

The subject of the reports upon rails was taken up and Mr. Williams was placed upon the committee in place of Mr. Felton, who has resigned.

Mr. Higginson called the attention of the association to the switch invented by Mr. Hall, which was commended for the ingenuity of the arrangement of the different parts.

The subject of advertising the rules and regulations was called up by Mr. Twichell and after some discussion it was

Voted—

That the rules and regulations be published one month in the "Daily Atlas" and that the Secretary be directed to keep the same constantly in one daily paper published in Boston.

The subject of baggage returns was taken up and after some discussion it was moved by Judge Gove, and

Voted—

That fifty cents fine be assessed upon each member of the association, who fails to return the baggage on hand each month, and the Secretary be directed to give notice of the same to each member.

On motion of Mr. Twichell.

Voted—

That a committee be appointed to draft a form for receipt for merchandise, and submit the same at the next meeting, in order if possible that a common form of receipt may be used by all the roads.

Mr. Higginson was appointed on this committee.

Voted—

That a committee consisting of the President and Mr. Higginson be instructed to examine the rules and regulations and report to the association at the next meeting if in their opinion any amendment is required in them.

The subject of discussion: "System of ticket accountability," was laid over for the next meeting of the association.

WM. P. PARROTT.

THIRD MONTHLY MEETING, 1851.

Third monthly meeting was held in Boston, March 19th, 1851.

Present:

Messrs. Higginson.
Jas. Moore.
Stearns.
Southwick.
Williams.
Twichell.
Hale.
Tilton.
Bourne.
Bigelow.   (10)

The President and Vice President being absent, Mr. Higginson was chosen chairman.

The record of the last meeting was read and approved.

Communications were received and read from Mr. Tyng of Lowell, in relation to an improved method of fitting tires to wheels; referred to the Secretary.

From Mr. Mowry with a specimen of an improved car coupling.

The Secretary presented a report upon Myer's patent slide table, which was read and accepted.

Mr. Southwick moved the reconsideration of the vote for advertising the rules and regulations in the Boston papers and made some remarks in relation to roads not terminating in Boston. After some discussion and explanations the subject was laid upon the table.

The subject for discussion was then taken up and remarks made upon the same by several members, but no further action taken upon it.

Voted—

That the subject for discussion for the next meeting be: "The Legislative returns."

FOURTH MONTHLY MEETING, 1851.

The fourth monthly meeting was held at the room of the association in Boston, on Wednesday, April 23, 1851.

Present:

Messrs. Lee.

Nelson.

Southwick.

Tilton.

Bigelow.

Twichell.

Merritt.

Williams.

S. T. Corser.

James Sweetsir.

Pickering.   (12)

The record of the last meeting was read and approved.

Mr. Henry Gray, Supt. of the Western railroad, was elected an immediate member.

Notice was received from Mr. Hunt and from Mr. Atkinson that they had resigned their offices as Superintendents of rail roads.

Mr. Nelson proposed Mr. Hunt as an associate member.

The Secretary presented for examination the pattern of a chair designed by S. Ashburner, Esqr., civil engineer of Boston.

Also—

A new mode of coupling the bell rope of a train invented by Mr. Ware of Warren, R. I.

Mr. Williams nominated S. S. Simmons, Supt. of the   . . .

Voted—

That the Secretary purchase the volumes of rail road charters and laws lately published in Boston.

Report upon Turner's patent was laid over to next meeting.

Report upon Tyngs' plan for fitting tires was read and laid upon the table.

On motion of Mr. Southwick it was

Voted—

That the next meeting of the association be held at Taunton.

Adjourned.

SEVENTH MONTHLY MEETING, 1851.

The seventh monthly meeting, 1851, was held at the association rooms, Boston, on Wednesday, July 23d, 1851.

Present:

Messrs. Lee.	Gove.
Higginson.	Haven.
Williams.	Bourne.
Tilton.	Swasey.
Hinkley.	(12)
Twichell.	
Southwick.	
Stearns.	
Nelson.	

Record of last meeting was read and approved.

Mr. Hunt was elected an associate member.

Mr. S. Simmons was elected an immediate member.

Mr. Higginson presented a track signal used by track repairers on the Lowell rail road.

Secretary presented a communication from Mr. Felton in relation to cast iron tires for driving wheels which was read and placed on file with the report upon Mr. Tyng's plan for setting tires.

An explanation was made by the President in relation to the change of the time for the meeting.

The committee upon Turner's patent presented their report which was read and accepted and upon motion of Mr. Higginson it was

Voted—

That the report embraces the views of the association upon that subject.

Voted—

.That the committee upon Turner's brake be instructed to consider also generally the fastening of brakes to cars now used.

The committee upon the subject of common form for receipts for merchandise asked for further time in which to report, and upon their motion it was

Voted—

That the Secretary insert a request in the next notices to the different Superintendents for a copy of the receipt now used and approved of by them.

Voted—

That the President, Mr. Gray and Mr. Twichell be a committee to investigate the claim of Septimus Norris for the patent right to use four eccentrics upon locomotive engines.

Voted—

That the next meeting be held at Portland, Maine, at 7 P. M., and that Mr. Williams and the Secretary be a committee to make the necessary arrangements.

EIGHTH MONTHLY MEETING, 1851.

The eighth monthly meeting was held on the 20th of August, A. D., 1851, at Portland, Maine.

Present:

Messrs. Lee.

Swasey.

Crocker.

Nelson.

Russell.

Sweetsir.

Bourne.

Tilton.

Haven.

Gove.

.Corser.

Williams.

Higginson.   (13)

The record of the last meeting was read and approved.

Secretary reported that he had collected a number of forms of receipts from different roads.

Mr. Williams presented a model for a new arrangement of of spiral springs for cars.

Committees on different subjects did not report.

A letter from Mr. Moore was presented by the President in relation to Turner's brake.

Ordered to be filed and it was

Voted—

That the Secretary send a copy of the same to Mr. Turner.

Voted—

That the subject of "Conductors carrying money" be attended to and that the Secretary make a memorandum of the same upon the record.

The President gave notice that he should call up at an early period the matter of requiring express men to give bonds to save rail road companies from loss through their default.

On motion of Mr. Higginson.

Voted—

That a committee of three be appointed to confer with the committee of the Mechanics Fair at Lowell, in relation to an exhibition of locomotive engines.

Committee, Messrs. Higginson,
Felton,
Parrott.

Voted—

That the association meet at Bristol ferry in R. I., on Thursday week.

Adjourned.

NINTH MONTHLY MEETING, 1851.

The ninth monthly meeting was held in Boston, on Wednesday, Sept. 10th, 1851.

Present:

Messrs. Lee.
Higginson.
Moore.
Bourne.
Tilton.
Upham.
Corser.
Pratt.
Stearns.
Hinkley.
Southwick.
Gove.   (12)

The record of the last meeting was read and approved.

The committee appointed at the last meeting to confer with the Mechanics Association at Lowell, in relation to a trial of locomotive engines. Reported

That they had agreed with the committee of that association that the judges should be nominated by the rail road association and be approved of by the Mechanic's association.

They also reported that in their opinion the association should assume the contingent expense of the experiments and that the requisite cars required should be contributed by the different roads.

On motion of Judge Upham.

Voted—

That the committee nominate a list of judges for the acceptance of this association, whereupon the committee nominated:

Capt. W. H. Swift, Boston,

Prof. Benj. Pierce, Cambridge,

Mr. Isaac Hinkley, Lowell,

Mr. Geo. W. Corliss of Providence,

Mr. W. P. Parrott of Boston,

which names were accepted.

On motion of Mr. Higginson.

Voted—

That the Secretary be authorized to expend a sum of money not exceeding five hundred dollars for the purpose of making the necessary arrangements for the proposed trial of locomotives on the Boston & Lowell rail road and Wilmington branch.

Voted—

That the committee nominate three other persons as substitutes in case of vacancy in the list of judges. The following gentlemen were nominated and accepted:

S. M. Felton.

Isaac Adams.

Simeon Borden.

Adjourned.

ANNUAL MEETING, JANUARY, 1852.

Annual meeting, Jany., 1852, was called in accordance with the Constitution on the first Wednesday in January.

In consequence of the heavy storm of snow, a quorum did not attend. The meeting, was, therefore, adjourned to the first Wednesday in February.

Attest.

WM. P. PARROTT,

Secy.

The adjourned annual meeting was held in Boston, according to adjournment on Wednesday 4th of February, at $7\frac{1}{2}$ P. M.

Present:

Messrs. Lee.

Higginson.

Twichell.

R. Hale.

Swasey.

Nelson.

Williams.

Haven.

Hinkley.

Southwick.

Bourne.

Tilton. (12)

The record of the last meeting was read and approved.

The Chair appointed Messrs. Bourne and Swasey, committee on accounts.

The association then proceeded to ballot for officers for the ensuing year, and

W. Raymond Lee was unanimously elected President.

Chas. F. Gove, Vice President.

W. P. Parrott, Secretary.

R. B. Mason, Esqr., was elected an associate member, he having resigned his office as Supt. Mr. Liberty Bigelow was likewise and for same reason elected an associate member.

Mr. I. S. Dunlap, nominated at a previous meeting at which no quorum was present and at which no record was made, was elected an immediate member, the association voting that the said nomination was valid.

Mr. Tilton nominated Geo. W. Whistler, Esqr., Supt. of the New York & New Haven rail road, as an immediate member.

The committee on accounts reported that they find the cash expenditures properly vouched.

Voted—

That a sixth assessment of ten dollars be laid and the Secretary be directed to collect the same.

Models were presented from Hinkley for improved six wheeled car truck.

F. A. Stevens patent brake. Specimens of wrought iron chairs from the Glendon iron company.

From Mr. Chs. F. Thomas, Taunton, a lithographic drawing of a locomotive engine, as a donation which was accepted.

Voted—

That the Secretary convey to Mr. Thomas the thanks of the association for his donation.

From Mr. Stanley of Troy, model of cast iron wheel.

On motion of Mr. Higginson.

Voted—

That a committee of three be appointed to report at the next meeting some plan for increasing the efficiency of the association both in its action and financies with power to confer with the Society of Civil Engineers upon the subject.

Messrs. Higginson,
        Tilton,
        Parrott,
were appointed.

On motion of Mr. Twichell.

A committee of three was appointed to consider the subject of allowing the Association of Machinists to occupy the rooms of this association at their meetings.

Messrs. Twichell,
        Bourne,
        Haven,
were appointed.

MONTHLY MEETING, MARCH 24TH, 1852.

Was duly held at the room of the association, No. 11½ Tremont row, at 7½ P. M.

Present:

Messrs. Lee.
        Corser.
        Dexter.
        Kinsman.
        Pickering.
        Sweetsir.
        Swasey.
        Twichell.
        Southwick.
        Gray.
        Stowell.
        Nelson.
        Higginson.
        Hinkley.   (14)

The record of the last meeting was read and approved.

Geo. W. Whistler, Esqr., Supt. N. Y. & N. H. R. R., was duly elected an immediate member.

Mr. Edwin Noyes, Supt. of the Androscoggin & Kennebec rail road, was proposed by Mr. Corser.

A communication was read from W. Parker, Esqr., in relation to the annual rail road reports of Massachusetts.

On motion of Mr. Southwick it was

Voted—

That a committee of five be appointed to take the same into consideration and to propose such amendments to the proper committee of the Legislature, to be adopted in the next year's returns after this year, the accounts for the present year being so far advanced.

This committee was nominated
Messrs. W. R. Lee.
       Southwick.
       Stowell.
       Kinsman.
       Parrott.

A car wheel model presented from Mr. Gardner, showing the construction adopted by the New York car wheel Co., having a wrought iron tire and cast iron disks. Geo. N. Phipps, No. 4 Albany block, agent.

A model of Mr. Landry's frog presented by Mr. Landry.

The committee for making a report upon the subject of increasing the efficiency of the association, made a verbal report in relation to the finances and recommended the following vote which was passed as follows:

Voted—

That the Secretary of the association notify all delinquent members of the association and rail way companies concerned of the amounts now due from them.

The committee further reported that they had made a proposition to the Socy. of Civil Engineers that they should occupy the rooms adjoining and that the libraries of the two societies should be united.

In consideration of the advantages which this association would derive from the joint use of the books and models belonging to that society and other advantages it was

Voted—

That the association contribute one hundred dollars towards the rent per annum of the adjoining room and for the considerations set forth in the report of the committee. The Secretary be authorized to pay the same and a sum not exceeding fifty dollars towards the expense of removal from the rooms now occupied by said Socy. of Civil Engineers.

Voted—

That the Secretary be authorized to subscribe to the English rail way times, and Herepath's rail way journal.

Adjourned.

MONTHLY MEETING, MAY 19TH, 1852.

Monthly meeting, May 19th, 1852, was held at the association rooms, at $7\frac{1}{2}$ P. M.

Present:

Messrs. Higginson.
        Corser.
        Williams.
        Bourne.
        Haven.
        Bigelow.
        Swasey.
        Nelson.
        Hinkley.
        Parrott.   (10)

The President and Vice President being absent, Mr. Higginson was chosen chairman.

The record of the last meeting was read and approved.

The govt. of the association announced the death of James Sweetsir, Esqr., Supt. of the Portsmouth, Portland and Saco rail roads, whereupon the following resolutions were presented and adopted by the association.

Resolved, that this association herewith deep regret the announcement of the death of our late brother member James Sweetsir, Esqr.

Resolved, that this association can with great justice bear witness of his modest worth, ability, and honesty of purpose, qualities which have made him to be esteemed by all the members of this association, and make his loss more deeply felt.

Resolved, that these resolutions be entered upon the records of the association.

The govt. announced a donation from the Hon. Abbott Lawrence, Minister to the Court of St. James, of a complete set of rail way reports.

The correspondence of his excellency with the departments in relation to the same being read it was

Voted—

That the thanks of this association be presented to the Hon. Abbott Lawrence for the very valuable collection of Parliamentary rail way reports procured from the English Government through his generous exertions.

Voted—

That in this act of Mr. Lawrence the association recognize with gratitude the continuance of that interest in the promotion of science, which on other occasions he has so munificently manifested.

The following candidates for membership were proposed.

W. S. Whitwell, Supt. of the Cheshire rail road, by Mr. Higginson.

Thos. H. Canfield, Supt. of the Rutland and Washington rail road, by Mr. Bigelow.

John B. Wyman, Supt. of the Connecticut river rail road, by Mr. Twichell.

P. R. Chandler, Supt. Vt. Valley R. R., by Mr. Williams.

Adjourned.

At this meeting a brake for cars used on the Reading rail road, illustrated with or by a fine model, was exhibited. It was generally considered too complicated for common use.

MONTHLY MEETING, AUGUST 26, 1852.

Was held at the Union house in Springfield, at 7½ P. M.

Present:

Messrs. Gove.   S. H. P. Lee.
        Williams.
        Stowell.
        Higginson.
        Southwick.
        Gray.
        Swasey.
        Twichell.
        Haven.
        Schlatter.
        Hinkley.
        Whistler.
        Nelson.
        Stearns.
        Hale.
        Chandler.
        Parker.
        Tilton.   (18)

The record of the last meeting was read and approved.

The association then proceeded to ballot for the admission of members previously nominated and the following members were elected:

P. R. Chandler, Supt. Vt. Valley rail road.

Edwin Noyes, Supt. Androscoggin & Kennebec R. R.

Thos. H. Canfield, Supt. Rutland and Washington.

John B. Wyman, Supt. Conn. R. R. R.

Mr. Whitwell having resigned his office as Supt. of the Cheshire rail road, his nomination was withdrawn.

Mr. Williams nominated Walter S. Johnson, Supt. of the Western Vermont rail road.

Mr. Higginson nominated Jos. A. Gilmore, Supt. of the Concord and Claremont rail road.

A communication was read from Jonathan Amory, Esqr., in relation to the furnaces of locomotive engines and economy in the consumption of fuel; referred to the committee on patents.

Mr. Higginson by request was excused from serving longer on the patent committee and Mr. Stowell was elected in his stead.

On motion by Mr. Higginson,

Voted—

That the Secretary notify to each member the names of the committee on patents.

Voted—

That the fine for non-return of baggage on hand be collected from all members who have failed to make such returns since January last.

On motion of Mr. Twichell,

Voted—

The Secretary notify each road to make return of baggage on hand on the first of September.

Voted—

That Mr. Twichell be a committee to consider the subject of said returns and report to the next meeting if some better plan can be derived to obtain lost baggage.

Voted—

That the Secretary be directed to collect the arrearages of subscription from the Concord road now due.

Adjourned.

MONTHLY MEETING, NOVEMBER 10TH, 1852.

Was held at the Massasoit house in Springfield, at 8 P. M.

Present:

Messrs. Lee.
       Tilton.
       Hale.
       Twichell.
       Schlatter.
       Gove.
       Whistler.
       Southwick.
       Gray.

Nelson.
Haven.
Swasey.
S. H. P. Lee.
Pratt.
Stowell.
Higginson.
Hinkley.
Dexter.
Dunlap.
Stearns.   (20)

The record of the last meeting was read and approved.

Walter S. Johnson, Supt. of the Western Vermont rail road, was elected an immediate member.

Joseph A. Gilmore, Supt. Concord & Claremont rail road, was elected an immediate member.

Mr. Tilton nominated E. A. Chapin, Supt. of the Cheshire rail road, as an immediate member.

Philo Hurd, Supt. of the Naugatuck rail road, nominated at the September meeting by Mr. S. H. P. Lee, at which meeting no record was made, was elected an immediate member.

The chairman of the committee on patents made a verbal report in relation to Ross Winans' claim for patent right in the eight wheel cars, giving his reasons for the opinion that there is a good defence against the same.

Mr. Twichell reported in relation to his plan for restoring lost baggage and freight.

That he had employed as an experiment Mr. Hayward to attend to this business and that he had commenced his operations in sending out notices, etc.

That the pay agreed upon was thirty-five dollars per month, no part of which was to be paid by any road unless the advantage to them may be evident.

On motion by Mr. Higginson,
Voted—

Whereas, the association approve of the action of the committee.

The committee be authorised to procure the publication of the name and address of the said agent in rail way guide.

After discussion on the subject of the report it was
Voted—

That the report be recommitted to a committee of three to report at the next meeting.

The Chair appointed as this committee:

Messrs. Twichell.

Higginson.

Tilton.

Mr. Higginson reported a general form for freight receipts, the consideration of which, owing to the lateness of the hour, was deferred to the next meeting.

Voted—

That the committee on patents report at the next monthly meeting upon Davenport's claim for side motion.

Landry's claim for an improvement in frogs for rail ways.

Mr. Pratt suggested that this invention was described in Wood's treatise on rail ways.

MONTHLY MEETING, DECEMBER 22D, 1852.

Was held at 11½ Tremont row, at 7½ P. M.

Present:

Messrs. Twichell.

Higginson.

Hinkley.

Nelson.

Gray.

Southwick.

Corser.

Bigelow.

Kinsman.

Williams.

Johnson.

Chandler.

W. S. Johnson.   (13)

R. Brainard, Esqr., Supt. Champlain & St. Lawrence.

The President and Vice President being absent Mr. Twichell was elected chairman.

The record of the last meeting was read and approved.

Mr. Chapin, Supt. Cheshire R. R., was elected a member.

The report of the committee on patents in relation to the claim of Davenport & Bridges and E. Landry was read and accepted, first erasing the word "safety" therefrom.

And the Secretary was directed to send a copy of the same to the Secretary of the general association.

Communications from G. W. Whistler, Esqr., in relation to Rice & Kimball's patent,

From the New York & Erie road in relation to Tanner's brake, etc., were referred to the committee on patents.

Communications from Mr. Tyng asking for information relative to the cost of maintaining the driving wheels of locomotives, was referred to Mr. Southwick.

The report of the committee on form for receipts was read and ordered to be printed.

On motion of Mr. Higginson it was

Voted—

That the proposition of the "Policy of paying ticket sellers and some other employees" by a commission be discussed at the next meeting.

WM. P. PARROTT.

ANNUAL MEETING, 1853.

The annual meeting of the association for the year 1853, was held according to adjournment from the first Wednesday of January (at which time no quorum was present) on Wednesday, Jany. 19th, at 11½ Tremont row, at 7½ P. M.

Present:

Messrs. Lee.
       Gove.
       Tilton.
       Bourne.
       Noyes.
       Bigelow.
       Williams.
       Twichell.
       J. S. Dunlap.
       Southwick.   (10)

The record of the last meeting was read and approved.

The association then proceeded to the election of officers for the ensuing year.

Mr. Lee declined a reelection as President.

C. F. Gove declined reelection as Vice President.

Upon the first ballot there was no election for President.

Mr. Lee again declined being considered a candidate and upon the second ballot L. Tilton was elected President for the ensuing year.

Upon the ballot for Vice President, Thos. S. Williams was elected.

Messrs. Southwick and J. S. Dunlap were appointed a committee to examine the accounts of the Secretary, who reported them correct.

Upon ballot for Secretary, W. P. Parrott was elected for ensuing year.

The annual meeting then adjourned.

Monthly Meeting, 1853.

The committee on patents reported verbally by the chairman, Mr. Lee, in relation to the contested rights for car brakes, viz., Turner's, Tanner's & Bachelder, Hodges' & Stevens's patents. That the committee do not agree in realtion to the principles involved and which are in fact questions of law and consequently not within the province of this committee to decide.

They, therefore, recommend that the association make no decision thereon by submitting a written report but that the several parties apply to the proper tribunals for the settlement of such cases.

In relation to the claim of Kimball & Rice for an improved method of hanging brakes, they are of opinion as at present informed that the claim is too broad inasmuch as the application of elastic substances for the same purpose was used prior to the date of their invention upon the northern road as they are informed by Mr. Stearns.

This part of the claim is therefore invalid and any road has a right to use elastic tubes round the link for hanging brakes without infringing this patent. In relation to the box which constitutes the other part of the patent they are not in possession of evidence to show that it is not new.

In the discussion which followed this report it was suggested that the box was substantially the same as a journal box and that the rubber or other elastic substance was the substantial part of the claim.

The report of the committee on common form for receipts was taken up and on motion by Mr. Twichell it was

Voted—

That the Secretary request of each road in the association an approval or disapproval of the same and in the latter case the objections to the proposed form.

Also that the Secretary ascertain what is the value of the present stock of printed receipts and what arrangement can be made to substitute the present form for them.

Mr. D. N. Pickering having notified the association that he had resigned his office as Superintendent of the Norfolk County road, he was unanimously elected an associate member.

App'd,

WM. P. PARROTT.

MONTHLY MEETING, MARCH, 1853.

The monthly meeting for March, 1853, was held at the rooms of the association on Wednesday the 23d, at 7½ P. M.

Present:

Messrs. Tilton.
Haven.
Swasey.
Twichell.
Russell.
Hinkley.
Higginson.
Schlatter.
Noyes.
Southwick.   (10)

The record of the last meeting was read and approved.

Communication from the Ohio Association was read and placed on file.

Report upon form of freight receipt was made, whereupon it was

Voted—

That the Secretary procure a plate proper for the head of the receipts and cause the same with the proposed form to be printed and furnish each road with twelve or more copies with the information that this association recommend the same for common use.

Mr. Imlay's communication in relation to his alleged patent claim with Mr. Felton's letter in relation to same was placed on file.

Voted—

That the Secretary cause an abstract to be made from the public returns of Mass., New York and New Hampshire and report the same to a committee consisting of Messrs. Southwick, Higginson, Twichell, Lee, Tilton and Parrott, who may cause the same to be printed.

Adjourned.

MONTHLY MEETING, APRIL, 1853.

The regular monthly meeting for April was held at the association rooms in Boston, on Wednesday the 20th, at 7½ P. M.

Present:

Messrs. Tilton.
  Lee.
  Twichell.
  S. H. P. Lee.
  Corser.
  Hale.
  Noyes.
  Dunlap.
  Swasey.
  Bigelow.
  Russell.
  Williams.
  Schlatter.
  Upham.
  Moore.
  Stearns.   (16)

The record of the last meeting was read and approved.

The Secretary reported a proof of the new freight receipts.

Reported also that the abstract of accidents was not prepared, not having the returns from New Hampshire.

A donation of a map from Col. Schlatter, drawn by Mr. Pelletier of the northern rail road, was received and it was

Voted—

That the thanks of the association be presented for the same, and that the Secretary cause the same to be properly framed and placed in the association room.

Mr. Williams nominated Charles S. Tenney, Supt. Newburyport R. R., and Jas. W. Emery, Portsmouth & Concord rail road, as immediate members.

The subject of strikes upon rail roads was introduced and discussed. Before action was had, the meeting adjourned.

WM. P. PARROTT,
Secy.

ANNUAL MEETING, 1854.

The annual meeting of the association for the year 1854, was held by adjournment on Wednesday evening, Jany. 18, at the rooms of the association, No. 11½ Tremont row, Boston.

Present:

Messrs. Williams.   Hyde.
  Swasey.

Moore.
Dunlap.
Stearns.
Twichell.
Hale.
Chandler.
Lee.
Hinkley.   (10)

The record of the last meeting was read and approved.

Messrs. Swasey and Dunlap were appointed committee on accounts.

The following gentlemen previously nominated, were elected immediate members, viz:

Charles S. Tenney, Newbury Port & Georgetown R. R.

Jas. W. Emery, Portsmouth & Concord R. R.

Danl. Nason, Boston & Providence R. R.

Edward C. Hyde, Kennebec & Portland R. R.

Geo. W. Bentley, Worcester & Nashua R. R.

The association then proceeded to the choice of officers for the ensuing year.

William Parker was unanimously elected President.

Thos. S. Williams, Vice President.

William P. Parrott, Secretary.

Messrs. Swasey and Dunlap, committee on accounts, reported that they had examined the Secretary's accounts and found them correct.

On motion by Mr. Twichell,

Voted—

That a committee of three be appointed to select, procure and present in the name of this association a suitable testimonial to Mr. Higginson as a mark of the esteem in which his services in behalf of this association are held by the members.

REGULAR MONTHLY MEETING, MARCH, 1854.

Was held at the association rooms, on Wednesday 15th, 1854.
Present:

Messrs. Parker.
        Hyde.
        Kinsman.
        Southwick.
        Corser.
        Twichell.

Chapin.

Dunlap.

Williams.

Nason.

Bigelow.

Emery.

Bentley.

Swasey.

Moore.

Ruggles, Vt. & Mass.

Roberts, Ft. agent, Portland, Montreal.

Mr. Whittimore, Prest. Fitchburg R. R.

Stearns.   (16)

Mr. Williams was chosen Secy. P. T.

The record of the last meeting was read and approved.

Geo. V. Hoyle, Supt. Ogdensburg rail road,

Otis E. Ruggles, Supt. Vermont & Mass.,

Gylis Merrill, Supt. Sullivan rail road, were elected members.

Mr. Geo. Stark, Supt. Nashua R. R., was proposed by Mr. Wm. Parker.

The committee reported that they had procured and presented a suitable testimonial to Mr. Higginson.

Mr. Twichell reported that Tanner's claim for a patent brake had been examined and had been submitted to Joel Giles for examination and opinion on the same. Also reported in relation to the Babitt metal in part. Also in relation to baggage agent.

Mr. Williams proposed the following alteration in the constitution, viz.:

ARTICLE IV. To change the word ten before immediate members to the word six. So that six members may constitute a quorum.

also in

ARTICLE VIII. To substitute the word "twelve" (Members) for the word "two-thirds."

Mr. Southwick moved that the chair appoint a committee of three to nominate standing committees for the present year.

This committee reported as follows:

On Periodicals:

Messrs. Parker.

Nason.

Parrott.

On Wear of Iron:
  Messrs. Williams.
         Twichell.
         Chapin.
         Bently.
         Gray.
On Patents:
  Messrs. Parker.
         Twichell
         Bigelow.
         Parrott.
         Gov. Navin.
On Lost Baggage:
  Messrs. Twichell.
         Stark.
         Ruggles.

Voted—

That the Secretary be requested to prepare a history of the association from its commencement to the present time to be submitted to the association for adoption and publication.

Adjourned.

Mr. Corser proposed Charles Morse, Supt. of the Androscoggin & Kennebec R. R., and J. S. Martin, Supt. of the Montreal district of the Grand trunk rail road.

MONTHLY MEETING, JULY 19, 1854.

A regular monthly meeting was held at Worcester (office of Nashua & Worcester R. R.) on Wednesday, July 19th, 1854.
Present.:

Messrs. Parker.
       Russell.
       Bentley.
       Swasey.
       Williams.
       Nason.
       Southwick.
       Twichell.
       Nelson.
       S. H. P. Lee.   (10)

Messrs. Stark of the Nashua R. R.; Kimball of the Cocheco R. R ; Morse of the Androscoggin & Kennebec R. R., were elected members of the association.

The committee on "presentation" reported, which report was accepted.

The letter of the committee and the reply of Mr. Higginson were ordered to be placed upon the record.

On motion of Mr. Williams it was

Voted—

That an assessment of ten dollars be laid upon each member of the association.

Adjourned.

WM. P. PARROTT,

Secy.

BOSTON, *March* 18, 1854.

DEAR SIR:

At the late annual meeting of the New England Association of Railroad Superintendents the definite intelligence of your having given up the idea of resuming your duties as Agent of the Lowell Railroad Company, was considered and the regrets of the members, both for the disappointment of your personal friends in general, and for your virtual separation from the association were feelingly exchanged.

The desire also prevailed to offer you a token of regards, which, while it should be as simple as possible, might yet be worthy to be kept constantly near you and remind from day to day of the esteem and respect of the members, who look back with so much pleasure to the monthly meetings they have enjoyed with you. It was therefore

Voted—

"That a committee of three be appointed, to select, procure and present in the name of the association a suitable testimonial to Mr. Higginson as a mark of the esteem in which his services in behalf of this association are held by the members."

As members of that committee we offer for your acceptance the accompanying pitcher and salver which we have selected as a very simple compliance with our instructions on this occasion.

We know very well, that it can only be under the conviction of the utmost sincerity of this offering, that you will find pleasure, in receiving it, and we beg to assure you of this in a manner that **has** no reserve.

The position you have deservedly held in the public estimation, we feel to have been an honor to us your associates, as your ever fervent zeal for the prosecution of the common objects and interests of the association were of the utmost *service* to us and we could not rest satisfied with ourselves, without thus acknowledging our obligations, by a token which shall follow you into your retirement where few of us will be favored with an opportunity otherwise to be borne in your remembrance.

We rejoice sincerely in the good tidings we receive of your comparative restoration, and we cherish the hope that if not allowed to mix again in the whirl of business cares and labors, you may under the blessing of God see many years of peaceful enjoyment, and be able to pursue the leadings of your good taste in all that improves the head or heart.

We remain, dear sir, most truly and affectionately,

.   YOUR FRIENDS.

BOSTON, *May 15th,* 1854.

WM. RAYMOND LEE.
WM. PARKER.
WM. P. PARROTT, ESQS., COMMITTEE.

GENTLEMEN:

I received on Saturday last, a pitcher and salver, presented by the New England Association of R. R. Superintendents, together with your letter accompanying the gift.

I am at a loss for words fitly to do justice to my feelings so unexpected and undeserved a testimonial of the regard of the association.   And I feel doubly unable to respond suitably in view of the very kind note with which you were pleased to accompany the token.

This present, of whose beauty any one might be proud, must ever have to my eyes a significance more valued than beauty, by reminding me of friends and associates, with whom I have passed many hours of happy intercourse, whether in social enjoyment or in the pleasures of working together for the furtherance of the great interests intrusted to us.

Be assured that I must always look to those hours as among the happiest of my life, so I shall always treasure this beautiful gift, and be grateful for the kindness which prompted it.

Be pleased, Gentlemen, to convey to the Association, one and all my most heartfelt thanks, and the assurance that I must ever cherish for it the warmest interest.

And will you be kind enough to accept for yourselves, my very grateful and cordial regard and believe me

Very truly and affy.

Yours,

(Signed.)   WALDO HIGGINSON.

1855.

The annual meeting by adjournment and the regular monthly meeting were held on Wednesday, January the 24th, at 7½ P. M., in the rooms of the association in Boston.

Present:

Messrs. Parker.
Haven.
Bourne.
Nason.
Williams.
Southwick.
Kinsman.
Tenny.
Stark.
Bigelow.
Twichell.   (11)
Associates Nelson.
Hinkley.   (2)

The meeting was called to order at half past seven, the President in the chair.

Mr. D. L. Davis, road master of the Providence rail road, presented (by the Secy.) a cast iron joint chair fitted with rubber which had been in use one year.

On motion of Mr. Southwick it was

Voted—

That the association now proceed to the choice of officers for this year.

The chair appointed:

Messrs. Williams,
Southwick,
Stark,

as a committee to correct, sort and count the votes for officers.

The whole number of votes for President was ten, all of which were for William Parker, President.

The whole number of votes for Vice President was ten, all of which were for Genery Twichell, Vice President.

The whole number of votes for Secretary was eleven, all of which were for Wm. P. Parrott, Secretary.

On motion of Mr. Southwick the chair appointed Messrs. Williams and Kinsman committee on accounts.

On motion of Mr. Williams it was

Voted—

That the day and hour for future monthly meetings until otherwise ordered be the last Tuesday of the month, at 2 o'clock P. M.

Mr. P. St. M. Andrews, Supt. of the Norwich and Worcester rail road, was elected a member of the association.

On motion of Mr. Southwick the chair appointed

Messrs. Southwick,
          Haven,
          Stark,

Committee to nominate standing committees and the following were nominated and appointed.

Committee on Periodicals:

Messrs. Parker.
          Nason.
          Parrott.

Committee on Wear of Iron:

Messrs. Williams.
          Twichell.
          Chapin.
          Bently.
          Gray.

Committee on Patents:

Messrs. Parker.
          Twichell.
          Bigelow.
          Parrott.
          Haven.

Committee on Lost Baggage:

Messrs. Twichell.
          Stark.
          Ruggles.

Mr. Williams proposed James M. Whiton, Agent B. C. & M. R. R., as an immediate member.

On motion of Mr. Williams it was

Voted—

That absent members may vote by proxy upon the matter of the proposed change in the constitution provided the said change be notified in the notice of the next meeting.

Moved by Mr. Twichell—

That the 4th Article of the Constitution of the association be amended by substituting seven instead of ten immediate members shall form a quorum.

On motion of Mr. Stark

Voted—

That when this meeting adjourn it be to the last Tuesday in February.

Adjourned.

W. P. P.

MONTHLY MEETING, MARCH, 1855.

The monthly meeting for March, 1855, was held at the Association Rooms in Boston, Tuesday 27th, 1855.

Present:

Messrs. Parker.

Bourne.

Bigelow.

Bently.

Twichell.

Stark.

Haven.

Proxies:

Messrs. Corser.

Russell.

Harris.

Nason.

Swasey.

Chapin.

Mathews.

Merrill.

Chandler.

On the question of amendment to the constitution, sixteen members, being two-thirds, were present and voted.

The Yeas and Nays were called as above and was declared to be a vote.

James M. Whiton, Agent R. C. & M. R. R. Co.. was elected an immediate member.

Mr. Bourne proposed Horace Scott, Supt. of the Fair Haven Branch R. R., as an immediate member.

Mr. Haven proposed John B. Winslow, Supt. of the Providence & Worcester R. R., as an immediate member.

MONTHLY MEETING, JULY, 1855.

The monthly meeting for July, 1855, was held on the 24 inst., at Bellows Falls.

Present:
Messrs. Parker.
       Bigelow.
       Stark.
       Chapin.
       Chandler.
       Merrill.
       Ruggles.
       Williams.
       Bentley.   (9)

Mr. Horace Scott of the Fair Haven branch and Mr. John B. Winslow of the Providence and Worcester road were elected members.

The following gentlemen were proposed:

Mr. Nourse, Salem & Lowell road.

J. B. Baker, Troy & Rutland road.

Hoyt, New Haven & New York road.

Sherburne, Vt. Central road.

S. Ashburner, Providence & Hartford road.

J. L. Briggs, Conn. river road.

E. M. Read, Hartford & Springfield road.

Mr. Williams moved to amend the fourth article of the constitution, by striking out the part relating to the balloting for admission and inserting the following words "all persons acting permanently as superintendents of rail roads may become *ex-officio* members of this association upon signing the constitution.

Which motion was laid over under the rule and the Secretary instructed to give the required notice of the same.

Voted—

That the next meeting of the association be at Centre harbor, on the 25th of September next, at 6 P. M.

Voted—

That the Secretary give notice of the special subjects to come before the next meeting, viz:

Economy of fuel and oil, and that he request all the members to communicate such facts or views in relation to the same as they may have and to forward the same to the Secy. on or before the 20th of September.

Adjourned.

                        WM. P. PARROTT.

REGULAR MONTHLY MEETING, 1855.

The regular monthly meeting was held October 30th, at Boston, 2 o'clock P. M.

Present:

Messrs. Parker.   Noyes..
        Bigelow.
        Corser.
        Stark.
        Winslow.
        Williams.
        Ruggles.
        Bentley.   (9)

The record of the last meeting was read and accepted.

There having been no quorum at Centre harbor on the 25th of Sept., the vote on the amendment of the constitution was passed to this meeting. On motion of Mr. Bentley the amendment was adopted by the unanimous vote of the members present and by the written assent of the following members not present, but voting by proxy.

Messrs. Merrill.
        Chandler.
        Mathews.
        W. Canfield.
        Swasey.
        Bourne.

The meeting then adjourned.

WM. P. PARROTT,
Secy.

MONTHLY MEETING, NOVEMBER, 1855.

The regular monthly meeting for November, 1855, was held on Tuesday the 27th, at 2 o'clock P. M., at the association rooms in Boston.

Present:

Messrs. Parker.
        Swasey.
        Bourne.
        Haven.
        Perkins, Gt. Falls road.
        Prescott.
        Merritt.   (7)

The record of the last meeting was read and approved.

The President introduced the subject of rails and made some remarks upon the subject, calling the attention of the members present to the model of splice patented by Maj. Trimble and now used upon the Lowell road.

This subject was laid upon the table and on motion of Mr. Haven of the Old Colony road, it was

Voted—

That a committee of one be appointed to call the attention of the several roads to the prices to be charged to members of the Legislature.

And Mr Haven was appointed by the chair as this committee.

Upon the subject of rails it was

Voted—

That the Secretary address a communication to the Presidents and Superintendents of the several rail roads calling their attention to the subject of rails and that he call a meeting at some convenient time for the consideration of the subject.

Voted—

That the subject of Maj. Trimble's splice be referred to the committee on patents with instructions that they inquire into and report the validity of the same.

Voted—

That when we adjourn it be to the 18th of December.

Adjourned.

W. P. PARROTT,

Secy.

ANNUAL MEETING, 1856.

Annual meeting, A. D., 1856, by adjournment and regular monthly meeting for January, was held in Boston, at the association rooms, on Tuesday, January 29th, at 2 o'clock P. M.

Present:

Messrs. Twichell.
         Stark.
         Bigelow.
         Bentley
         Ruggles.
         Stearns.
         Parker.   (7)

Record of the last meeting read and approved.

The committee on accounts reported that they had examined the accounts of the Secretary and found them correct.

The association then proceeded to the election of officers for this year.

Genery Twichell, Supt. Boston and Worcester rail road, was unanimously elected President.

Geo. Stark, Lowell and Nashua rail road, Vice President.

Wm. P. Parrott, Secretary.

Messrs. Bigelow and Bentley were appointed committee on accounts for this year.

Voted—

That the next monthly meeting of the association be held on the last Tuesday in February, at 7 o'clock P. M.

WM. P. PARROTT,

Secy.

MONTHLY MEETING, FEBRUARY 26TH, 1856.

The regular monthly meeting of the association was held Tuesday, February 26th, at 7 o'clock P. M.

Present:

Messrs. Twichell.

   Stark.

   Stearns.

   Taber.

   Andrews.

   Bentley.

   Nason.

   Prescott.

   Winslow.

   Williams.

   Nelson.   (11)

The record of the last meeting was read and approved.

Messrs. Lee,

   Higginson,

   Parker,

   Williams,

   Southwick,

Were elected associate members.

The following committees were appointed.

On Periodicals:

Messrs. Stark.

   Nason.

   Parrott.

On Lost Baggage:
  Messrs. Haven.
        Ruggles.
        Taber.
On Rails:
  Messrs. Williams.
        Parker.
        Bentley.
        Chapin.
        Gray.
On Patents:
  Messrs. Parrott.
        Lee.
        Stearns.
        Haven.
        Winslow.
On Wheels and Axles:
  Messrs. Stark.
        Winslow.
        Prescott.
        Andrews.
        Bigelow.

The following resolution was passed.

Resolved, that each rail road Supt. in New England be requested on the first day of every month to take measures to ascertain the number of all foreign merchandise cars on his road and report the same to the Supt. of the road to which they belong.

Voted—

That the Secretary cause a copy of the above resolution to be sent to each rail road Supt. in New England.

On motion of Mr. Bentley, it was

Voted—

That hereafter the regular monthly meeting be held on the last Tuesday of each month, at 7 o'clock P. M.

Adjourned.

MONTHLY MEETING, MARCH 25TH, 1856.

Was held at Boston, at the rooms of the association, 7½ o'clock P. M.

Present:

  Messrs. Twichell.
        Bigelow.

Bentley.
Stark.
Greene.
Nason.
Andrews.
Swasey.

Communication from J. B. Felt, Secy. of the Dartmouth college association, asking for the use of the association rooms for their quarterly meeting, was read and referred to the Prest. and Secy. with full power to act.

Communication from Mr. Snow in relation to rail road advertising was read and it was

Voted—

That the Prest., Mr. Bigelow, Mr. Parrott, be a committee to prepare a plan and send a copy of the same to the rail road Presidents interested in the same.

Voted—

That the committees be notified and list of committee to be sent to each committee man.

Adjourned.

MONTHLY MEETING, APRIL 29TH, 1856.

Present:

Messrs. Twichell.
Stark.
Stearns.
Bigelow.
Bentley.
Andrews.
Parker.
Williams.
Rolfe.

There being no business before the meeting a general discussion was had upon matters of common interest.

The Secretary was not present at this meeting.

MONTHLY MEETING, JUNE 25TH, 1856.

Present:

Messrs. Twichell.
Taber.

Winslow.
Bentley.
Andrews.
Williams.
Swasey.   (7)

The record of the last meeting was read and accepted.

Reports were called for from the chairmen of different committees and verbal reports of progress made.

After some discussion of the subject of the difficulties attending the progress of the association in usefulness, its importance, and the mode by which reliable information may be obtained.

On motion of Mr. Swasey, it was

Voted—

That the government of the association prepare a memorial, to be sent to the different roads, asking of all the rail roads in New England, aid and cooperation in forwarding the objects of this organization.

Voted—

That the next regular meeting be at Springfield, Mass.

ANNUAL MEETING, JANUARY 7TH, 1857.

N. E. Association of R. R., Supts.   Annual meeting, January 7th, 1857, held at Boston, 7 o'clock P. M.

Present:

Messrs. Twichell.
        Stark.
        Winslow.
        Taber.
        Andrews.
        Bentley.
        Phillips.
Associates Parker.
        Southwick.

The meeting was addressed by the Prest., in relation to the continuance of the association and it was voted unanimously, that it is expedient and necessary that the association be preserved and continued.

Messrs. Stark and Taber were appointed the committee to audit the Secretary's accounts, who subsequently examined and reported that they were correct.

The Association then proceeded to the election of officers for the present year and the following were unanimously elected, viz:

President, Genery Twichell.

Vice President, George Stark.

Secretary, Wm. P. Parrott.

The President made a statement in relation to lost baggage and it was

Voted—

That the President and Secretary be a committee to report upon the subject of lost baggage agent and his compensation.

Mr. Parker made some remarks upon the subject of rails and it was voted that the Secretary be requested to ask Mr. Thos. S. Williams to prepare a paper upon this subject.

Upon the subject of patents applicable to rail roads it was

Voted—

That the Secretary prepare an abstract and report upon that subject.

Voted—

To adjourn to meet again upon notice from the govt. of the association.

WM. P. PARROTT,
Secy.

NEW ENGLAND ASSOCIATION.

Special meeting, May 26, 1857, at Boston, 3 P. M.

Present:

Messrs. Twichell.
Stark.
Winslow
Taber.
Merritt.
Prescott.
Stearns.
Gray.
Bentley.
Andrews.
Chapin.
Scott.   (12)

The Secretary submitted his report upon patents which was read and accepted.

On motion of Mr. Andrews it was

Voted—

That the report be printed under the direction of the Secretary.

On motion of Mr. Taber it was

Voted—

That the Secretary be requested to investigate and report the facts relative to Imlay's claim.

Voted—

To adjourn to the last Tuesday in June.

W. P. PARROTT,

Secy.

NEW ENGLAND ASSOCIATION OF RAIL ROAD SUPERINTENDENTS.

Monthly meeting, June 30th, 1857. Held at Boston.

Present:

Messrs. Stark.

> Andrews.
> Taber.
> Stearns.
> Williams.
> Rice, Prest., W. & N. R. R.
> Winslow.
> Adams, M. M., B. & W. R. R.
> A Brewster, Prest., N. & W. R. R.

The report on Imlay's patent was read.

The following resolve proposed by Mr. Rice, President of the Worcester and Nashua road, was passed unanimously.

Resolved, that a committee consisting of the President, Vice President and Secretary of the Association be appointed to take in charge the matter of the claims now made under the Imlay's patent, so called, and that the said committee be authorized to obtain such legal advice as they may deem necessary for a full recommendation and report to the association at an early day on the question of the validity of the said claim.

Adjourned.

W. P. PARROTT,

Secy.

NEW ENGLAND ASSOCIATION OF RAIL ROAD SUPERINTENDENTS.

Monthly meeting, July, 1857. Held at Boston.

Present:

Messrs. Twichell.

> Stark.
> Williams.

Bentley.

Taber.

Winslow.

The committee on Imlay's patent reported that in the opinion of counsel, competent to decide the proper course for rail road companies to pursue, is to defend against the alleged claim of Richard Imlay.

Because railroad companies do not use the arrangement described in said Imlay's patent and the question involves a principle, which abandoned, would open a wide door for the admission of implied claims against the rail roads.

The Secretary reported progress in the investigation of Mathews' claim for spark arrester.

Adjourned.

WM. P. PARROTT.

FINAL MEETING, JULY 29, 1857.

New England association of rail road Superintendents, July 29th, 1857.

At a special meeting called to consider the question of dissolving the association.

Present: Messrs. Stark, Swasey, Nason, Merritt, Phillips, and the Secretary; by letter Messrs. Stearns and Gilmore.

On motion of Mr. Swasey,

Voted—

That the association be dissolved on the 1st day of October, next and that the property of the association be left at the disposal of the government of the association.

Voted—

That the Secretary be directed to assess upon the subscribing roads a sufficient sum to pay the outstanding claims against the association.

Voted—

That Messrs. Merritt and Nason be a committee to audit the accounts of the Secretary and Treasurer and to certify the same if found to be correct.

Voted—

That the Secretary cause a copy of the proceedings of this meeting to be sent to each member of the association.

Voted—

To adjourn.

WM. P. PARROTT,

Secy.

ARTICLES OF CONSTITUTION.

1. Article First.

This association shall be called the New England association of rail road Superintendents.

2. Article Second.

The objects of the association shall be the increase and diffusion of knowledge upon scientific and practical subjects connected with rail roads and the promotion of harmony among the rail road companies of New England.

3. Article·Third.

It shall be composed of immediate and associate members. Immediate members shall be persons filling the office or discharging the duties of rail road Superintendents, in New England.

Any person may be chosen an associate member, whose connection with the association would tend to promote its objects.

4. Article Fourth.

Persons to be elected members, must be nominated at a regular meeting and balloted for at the next by the immediate members; a unanimous vote is necessary for a choice and the presence of as many as ten immediate members is necessary to constitute a regular meeting.

5. Article Fifth.

The association shall be regularly organized with a President, Vice President and Secretary, who shall be chosen by ballot by the immediate members.

The President and Vice President shall be chosen from among the immediate members.

The Secretary may be chosen from either the immediate or the associate members.

The regular time for the choice of officers shall be at the annual meeting on the first Wednesday in January. The officers for the present year shall be chosen at the meeting, at which these articles of constitution are accepted.

The duty of the President and in his absence of the Vice President shall be to preside at all meetings of the association.

The duty of the Secretary shall be to keep a record of the

proceedings of each meeting and to preserve all papers and other property belonging to the association.

He shall have charge of all ordinary business transaction, such as notifying members of meetings and making arrangements for the same.

He shall also act as treasurer, collect all assessments and pay all bills of the association and make a report at the annual meeting of his receipts and expenditures.

6. Article Sixth.

Meetings shall be held at such times and places and for such purposes in furtherance of the objects of the association as shall from time to time be determined.

And assessments, sufficient for the current expenses of the association, shall from time to time be laid upon all members, payable quarterly.

7. Article Seventh.

Each immediate member shall be at liberty to introduce one stranger at any meeting of the association.

8. Article Eighth.

This constitution may be at any time amended by the vote of two-thirds of the immediate members; the amendment having been proposed at the regular meeting previous to that at which it was voted upon.

9. Article Ninth.

Such of the following persons are to be considered original immediate members as intimate to the Secretary a wish to become so and sign the articles of constitution during the present year, viz: Wm. Raymond Lee, Supt. Boston and Providence rail road; James Barnes, Supt. Western rail road; Charles Minot, Supt. Boston and Maine rail road; Saml. M. Felton, Supt. Fitchburg rail road; Waldo Higginson, Agent Boston and Lowell rail road; William Parker, Supt. Boston and Worcester rail road; Joseph H. Moore, Supt. Old Colony rail road; N. G. Upham, Supt. Concord rail road; Chs. F. Gove, Supt. Lowell and Nashua rail road; Onslow Stearns, Agent, Northern rail road; John Russell, Jr., Supt. Portsmouth, Portland and Saco rail road; Isaac Hinkley,

Supt. Providence and Worcester rail road; S. H. P. Lee, Supt. Norwich and Worcester rail road; Wm. A. Crocker, Supt. Taunton & New Bedford rail road; George Haven, Supt. Fall River rail road; Luther Haven, Cape Cod Branch rail road; Lucian Tilton; Josiah Hunt, Supt. Connecticut river rail road; E. H. Brodhead, New Haven, Hartford and Springfield rail road.

Waldo Higginson

Emery Twichell

Geo. Stark

S. H. Tabor

Daniel Nason

John B Winslow

S. W. Bentley

A. S. M. Andrews.

Jere Prescott

NAMES OF ALL RECORDED MEMBERS AND OF THE RAILROADS REPRESENTED BY THEM.

Amy, F, Superintendent, New York, Providence & Boston R.R.
Andrews, P. St. M., Superintendent, Norwich & Worcester R.R.
Ashburner, S., Superintendent, Providence & Hartford R.R.
Atkinson, Theo., Superintendent, Manchester & Lawrence R.R.

Baker, J. B., Superintendent, Troy & Rutland R.R.
Barnes, Jas., Superintendent, Western R.R.
Bentley, Geo. W., Superintendent, Worcester & Nashua R. R.
Bigelow, Liberty, Superintendent, Rutland & Burlington R.R.
Bourne, Sylvanius, Superintendent, Cape Cod Branch R.R.
Brainard, E. H., Superintendent, Champlain & St. Lawrence R.R.
Briggs, J. L., Superintendent, Connecticut River R.R.
Brodhead, E. H., Superintendent, New Haven, Hartford & Springfield R.R.

Canfield, Thos. H., Superintendent, Rutland & Washington R.R.
Chandler, P. R., Superintendent, Vermont Valley R.R.
Chapin, E. A., Superintendent, Cheshire R.R.
Chesborough, E. S.
Corser, Solomon T., Superintendent, Atlantic & St. Lawrence R.R.
Crane, Edward.
Crocker, Wm. A., Superintendent, Taunton & New Bedford R.R.

Dexter, Geo. W.
Dunlap, J. S.

Elkins, James N., Superintendent, Boston, Concord & Montreal R.R.
Emery, Jas. W., Superintendent, Portsmouth & Concord.

Farnum, Henry, Superintendent, New Haven & Northampton R.R.
Felton, Samuel M. (Sr.), Superintendent, Fitchburg R.R.
Follett, Timothy, Superintendent, Rutland & Burlington R.R.

Gage, D. A., Superintendent, Sullivan R.R.
Gilmore, Joseph A, Superintendent, Concord & Claremont R.R.
Gove, Chas. F., Lowell & Nashua R.R.
Gray, Henry, Superintendent, Western R.R.

Hale, Robert, Superintendent, Connecticut & Passumpsic Rivers R.R.
Harris, Elbridge, Superintendent, Bangor & Piscataqua Canal and R.R.
Haven, George, Superintendent, Fall River R.R.
Haven, Luther, Superintendent, Cape Cod Branch R.R.
Higginson, Waldo, Agent, Boston & Lowell R.R.
Hinckley, Isaac, Superintendent, Providence & Worcester R.R.
Hoyle, G. V., Superintendent, Ogdensburg R.R.
Hoyt, —, Superintendent, New Haven & New York R.R.
Hunt, Josiah, Superintendent, Connecticut River R.R.
Hurd, Philo, Naugatuck R.R.
Hyde, Edward C., Superintendent, Kennebec & Portland R.R.

Johnson, S. F., Superintendent, Vermont & Massachusetts R.R.
Johnson, W. R., Superintendent, Western Vermont R.R.
Jones, D. S., Superintendent, Vermont & Massachusetts R.R.

Kimball, —, Superintendent, Cocheco R.R.
Kinsman, John, Superintendent, Eastern R.R.
Kirkwood, Jas. P., Superintendent, New York & Erie Ry.

Lee, S. H. P., Superintendent, Norwich & Worcester R.R.
Lee, Wm. Raymond, Superintendent, Boston & Providence R.R.

Mahan, Prof. D. H., West Point Academy.
Martin, J. S., Superintendent, Montreal District Grand Trunk Ry.
Mason, R. B., Superintendent, New York & New Haven R. R.
Mathews, A. S., Superintendent, New York, Providence and Boston R.R.
Merrill, Giles, Superintendent, Sullivan R.R.
Merritt, Wm.,Superintendent, Essex R.R.
Minot, Chas., Superintendent, Boston & Maine R.R.
Moore, James, Superintendent and Engineer, Vermont Central R.R.
Moore, Joseph H., Superintendent, Old Colony R.R.
Morse, Charles, Superintendent, Androscoggin & Kennebec R.R.

Nason, Daniel, Superintendent, Boston & Providence R.R.
Nelson, H. W., Superintendent, Norfolk County R.R.
Nourse, —, Superintendent, Salem & Lowell R.R.
Noyes, E., Superintendent, Androscoggin and Kennebec R.R.

Page, J. A., Superintendent, Connecticut & Passumpsic Rivers R.R.
Palmer, John W., Superintendent, New London, Willimantic & Palmer R.R.
Parker, Wm., Superintendent, Boston & Worcester R.R.
Parrott, Wm. P., Secretary of the Association.
Pickering, D. N., Superintendent, South Reading R.R.
Pond, Chas. F., Superintendent, Springfield & New Haven R.R.
Pratt, T. Willis, Civil Engineer.
Prescott, Josiah.

Read, E. M., Superintendent, Hartford & Springfield R.R.
Ruggles, B. C., Superintendent, Connecticut and Passumsic Rivers R.R.
Ruggles, Otis T., Superintendent, Vermont & Massachusetts R.R.
Russell, John, Jr., Superintendent, Portland, Saco & Portsmouth R.R.

Schlatter, C. L., Superintendent, Ogdensburgh R.R.
Scott, Horace, Superintendent, Fair Haven Branch R.R.
Sherburne, —, Superintendent, Vermont Central R.R.
Southwick, I. H., Superintendent, Providence & Worcester R.R.
Stark, George, Superintendent, Nashua R.R.
Stearns, Onslow, Agent, Northern R.R.
Stowell, I. W., Superintendent, Worcester & Nashua R.R.
Swasey, A. E., Superintendent, Taunton Branch R.R.
Sweetser, James, Superintendent, Portland, Saco & Portsmouth R.R.

Tabor, S. H.
Tenney, Charles F., Superintendent, Newburyport & Georgetown.
Tilton, Lucian, Civil Engineer, Cheshire R.R.
Twitchell, Genery, Superintendent, Boston & Worcester R.R.

Upham, N. G., Superintendent, Concord R.R.

Whistler, Geo. W., Superintendent, New York & New Haven R.R.
Whiton, James M., Superintendent, Boston, Concord & Montreal R.R.
Whitwell, W. S., Superintendent, Cheshire R.R.
Williams, Thos. S., Superintendent, Sullivan R.R.
Winslow, John B., Superintendent, Providence & Worcester R.R.
Wyman, John B, Superintendent, Connecticut River R.R.

SUBJECT INDEX.

CPSIA information can be obtained
at www.ICGtesting.com
Printed in the USA
BVHW04*1111170918
527708BV00014B/1834/P